THE 21ST CENTURY GENERALS

The Wilderness Experience

by

Gabriel Donkor

THE 21ST CENTURY GENERALS

Copyright © 2020 by Gabriel Donkor

Publisher
LAING Publishing
www.laingpublishing.com

Second Edition
ISBN-13: 978-1-7338772-2-0 - E-book
ISBN-13: 978-1-7338772-3-7 - Paperback

Printed in the United Kingdom and the United States of America

Unless otherwise stated, all scripture quotes are taken from the **New King James Version**; *with emphasis added or paraphrased.*

Publishing Consultants
Vike Springs Publishing Ltd.
www.vikesprings.com

For further information or to contact Gabriel please send an email to: gabriel@laingpublishing.com, angel24us@yahoo.com

Gabriel's books are available at special discounts when purchased in bulk for church groups or as donations for educational, inspirational and training purposes.

Limited Liability

This publication is designed to provide accurate and authoritative information in regard to the subject matter covered. It is sold with the understanding that the publisher and author are not engaged in rendering physiological, financial, legal or other licensed services. The publisher and the author make no representations or warranties with respect to the completeness of the contents of this work. If expert assistance or counselling is needed, the services of a specific professional should be sought. Neither the publisher nor the author shall be liable for damages arising here from. The fact that an organization or website is referred to in this work as a citation and/or a potential source of further information does not mean that the author or the publisher endorses the information that the organization or website may provide or recommendations it may make, nor does the cited organization endorse affiliation of any sort to this publication. Also, readers should be aware that due to the ever-changing information from the web, Internet websites and URLs listed in this work may have changed or been removed. All trademarks or names referenced in this book are the property of their respective owners, and the publisher and author are not associated with any product or vendor mentioned.

Dedication

To a Darling, Loving and wonderful woman of Excellence, Grace and Favor, my companion and helpmate who has inspired me with her love and prayers, Priscilla Jehu-Appiah Donkor. And to all women who has faith and look to the potentials and the future of the people they come across rather than what they have in their present to offer. To all such people, this book is dedicated to you

Ayekoo!!!

Table of Contents

Acknowledgements

I am extremely thankful for the insights and contributions that a variety of people made to this book. In particular, I am indebted to my wife, Priscilla Jehu-Appiah Donkor, whose persistence and donation of a laptop before we got married enabled me to shape my ideas and structure the materials gathered. You are such a darling!!!

Also, I am grateful to Reverend Mrs. Ama Ofosu-Koranteng (South Africa) and Reverend Roland Owusu-Ansah for their time of review and input at the early stages. And to my sister, Mrs. Priscilla Frimpong (USA), for the painstaking arguments and time to proofread and offer opinions; know that I value your work.

To my family and readers and those who look forward to another script, this is the doing of the Lord, and it is marvelous in our sight.

Preface

I can recall vividly an incident in September 1996. A few days before I finished my polytechnic training, the Spirit of the Lord impressed on my heart to wait on Him for certain days. On the second day of the waiting, which was the 26th of September, 1996, He revealed to me the purpose of my journey. **"I will teach you the successes and the failures of my great men and women and how they endured their wilderness experience. Again I will show you what I consider as the greatest, and you will need to make this available to my people. You will need to go through the wilderness as well for this purpose."** Thus began the genesis of this book – my own wilderness experience.

It has been a period of mixed experiences but worth looking back upon. I failed to endure in certain situations, even though the Lord told me about them. Like the prophet Balaam, we are aware of what God wants us to do, but for the pressures around and other things, we go to Him again and again about the same thing. Yet in my weakness, the grace of God was made perfect, just as Apostle Paul said. I came to understand the lessons of the generals and why God chose to have them in history. They simply teach us the lessons of life and His ways.

In February of 2011, whilst on a family trip to South Africa, the voice of the Lord came to me once again in this passage of Isaiah 51:2-3: "*Look unto Abraham your father, and unto Sarah that bare you: for I called him alone, and blessed him, and increased him. For the LORD shall comfort Zion: he will comfort all her waste places; and he will make her wilderness like Eden, and her desert like the garden of the LORD; joy and gladness shall be found therein, thanksgiving, and the voice of melody.*"

And the Lord said to me, "The period is over and now is the time to share these experiences." This was after I had responded to His call to leave my office work and to trust Him for what He can do with my life. As humans, trusting and obeying God is sometimes difficult, especially when reasoning and logic is interpreted in the context of spiritual instruction. I have come so far I now understand God and what He can do.

Each day now is a new experience in God, and my greatest desire is to fulfill God's purpose in my life. There are many more lessons being learned by me in my walk with the Lord. As you read this material, may the Spirit of the Lord minister to you. And if you are going through or about to go through your own wilderness training, may you be known as a general in your generation!

We all ought to go through the wilderness, but it is not the end; rather, it is the means to the end of what God has in store for us – the promised land. Stay blessed as you fulfill your purpose and as you read this book.

Introduction

T he 21st Century Generals – or God's wilderness born – are men and women raised by God in the end time as deliverers of our families, communities, and nations, bringing to pass divine counsel and mandate on this planet, providing hope and future for our generation through God. For this purpose, we ought to learn and read and understand the lives of these men and their wilderness walk so as not to repeat their same mistakes, but rather to draw lessons out to help us facilitate what God is about to do and is doing in our time. According to the great English statesman, Winston Churchill, "Experience is the avoidance of repeating the mistake of the past."

The time is now, and the hour is here. It does not matter your background in terms of family lineage, position, and occupation. Regardless of who you are, the Lord is raising men and women of integrity who have been through the wilderness – or will be prepared to go through the wilderness – to use them in establishing His will and purposes in our generation. Again, the hour is *now*. From Australia to Asia, Africa to America, and all across the borders of Europe, a new breeze and waves of God's wilderness generals are being raised to perform the end time commission. It is as though the Lord is saying, "Your experience is enough for me to demonstrate my power through you." What remains is our willingness to yield to this call and to say: "God, use me to do it." The world is looking for more than signs and wonders to convince them of our God. The deteriorating and corrupting world is looking for men and women of integrity and a willingness to show godly character by their actions and deeds, to affect both the immediate and future generations.

According to one of Bishop T.D Jakes podcast message, life is too short to learn all experiences by yourself. It is in this light that we need to read and learn of other people's experiences in order to avoid their mistakes. We can learn from men who walked with God and achieved some measure of excellence worth noting. Their experiences sum up the lessons for our study. All these men have some form of uniqueness. God used them for specific and significant work and they lived to serve their generation.

It is becoming difficult for many Christians to live the Christian life, because many of us fail to endure our wilderness and learn lessons from our experiences. For this reason, we tend to think that what we may be going through at any point in time is something applicable only to us. The truth of the situation is that there is nothing new under the sun. (Ecclesiastes 1:9) What you are going through now was once someone else's experience; they left their footprints so that we could see them and not commit the same mistakes. I believe the Christian life is an easy one to lead… not easy in terms of no suffering and or going through difficulties in life, but an easy one because if we understand the journey and read, study, and learn from the experiences of our patriarchs, we will be able to please God who seeks for us to please Him in our lives. (Matthew 5:48)

The 21st Century Generals are men and women with great visions birthed in them for the showing forth of God's power and manifestation. These are men and women birthed with songs and prophetic writings. They are also preachers and workers of other disciplines, both secular and in the Christian world. If the world is looking forward for the prophetic word, Romans 8:19 says, *"For the earnest expectation of the creation awaits the manifestation of the sons of God."* There is coming a revival on and across the Earth. This revival – like the many others that have already taken place on the planet Earth – will be sustained and continued throughout the rest of the world until the coming of Christ.

It is therefore important for God to prepare men and women who have gone through their wilderness, learned their lessons well, and have the next generation in mind to make the next move... dreamers and vision possessors like Joseph; deliverers of oppressors like Moses; promise and covenant possessors like the Israelites; kings and queens after God's own heart like David; prayer warriors and men of excellent spirit like Daniel; salvation providers and liberators like the son of God, Jesus; and many others who went through their wilderness and came out tried and tested to make the purposes of God established through them.

I desire and pray always that God will make me the Joseph, Moses, David, Daniel and the Jesus of my generation in order to impact my generation with His potential. So do I desire that for you as a child of God.

What you may be doing, whether in secular or religious circles, is not the issue at stake, but instead your preparedness to be available for God's end time purposes – i.e., making available your testimonies, your wilderness experiences, to serve as lessons for others. It's time to show forth what you have desired to do for God for so long. The platform for you is where you find yourself now; God is not limited to using it to show forth His glory. I challenge you to be counted as a General of the 21st Century. Seek for the promotion as a soldier of God to the rank of a general. The rank of a general comes with a mark of distinction and hard work, and I believe you are certainly qualified to become one yourself.

In the theory of God, you can only be useful by Him if you learn to die to self and let Him live through you. You cannot serve Him better in Egypt. The call is to release you into the wilderness so that you can serve the great I AM. To come to the place of saying, "Here I am, Lord. Send me."

The call is to release you into the wilderness so that you can serve the great I AM. To come to the place of saying, "Here I am, Lord. Send me."

CHAPTER ONE

Why the Wilderness

. . . .

The essence of the wilderness experience is to learn how to obey God and follow Him. The consequence of it is the fruit of blessings and curses. God is not interested in sacrifices, but obedience.

. . . .

It is God's desire to bring His people to fulfill their destiny and to achieve His purpose for the human race. In order to accomplish this, He affords His children the opportunity of experiencing the wilderness life in order to perfect His will in them.

Many times, we think that our wilderness experience has no bearing on the plan of God for our life, especially when it is one of extreme difficulty. Notwithstanding this, there may be several reasons – known and unknown to us – that call for going through the wilderness.

"And it came to pass, when Pharaoh had let the people go, that God led them not through the way of the land of the Philistines, although that was near, for God said, Lest peradventure the people repent when they see war, and they return to Egypt. But God led

the people about, through *the way of the wilderness of the Red Sea: and the children of Israel went up harnessed from the land of Egypt."* (Exodus 13:17-18)

Wilderness Defined

The Greek word Tôhû *(to'-hoo)* refers to a desolation (of surface), that is, a desert; figuratively a worthless thing; adverbially in vain. It is a state of confusion, an empty place, without form; nothing.

"The wilderness" refers to a place of seclusion. It speaks of a period when you feel dry within and have nothing to offer, a place of discomfort and denial of the pleasures and the things in life that give you satisfaction.

Sometimes the wilderness represents the place where your heavens are shut over you. It becomes difficult to bear fruit in those periods in many areas of life, be it in your ministry, or your marriage, among others. (Jeremiah 51:43)

Reasons for the Wilderness

When the Lord was taking the Israelites from Egypt to the promised land, one of His purposes was to raise an army; so He decided to lead them through the wilderness. The rudiments of ground battles are better learned in the wilderness. As God's army (Ephesians 6:10), we go through the wilderness to be prepared and trained by God for the battles ahead, just as He led the Israelites.

The wilderness gives us the opportunity to be emptied of Egypt and be filled with the promise. In the Bible, Egypt is a symbol of worldly things that prevent and intimidate us from serving God. It is a place where we are made slaves to sin, just as the Israelites were slaves to the Egyptians. It is also a symbol of idolization. The wilderness is to facilitate the process of being emptied of Egypt in order to be filled with the good things of God.

> *God takes His children to the wilderness for them to get to know Him more and to seclude them for His divine appointment.*

God takes His children to the wilderness for them to get to know Him more and to seclude them for His divine appointment. In such moments, you feel deserted and lonely, but God never leaves you during that period.

Time in the wilderness affords us the opportunity to increase our love for God and get close to Him. God always seeks to establish a formidable relationship with us. Thus, when we are going through our wilderness, we should deem it fitting to tune in to more reading of His word and give ourselves to prayer for direction.

The wilderness is also a preparation period of a man before the appointed time. (Psalm 66:9-12) From this scripture, we understand that God causes us to go through the wilderness to be tried and refined as pure gold in order to bring us to our wealthy places – the promised land.

Many are those who are filled with worldly things such as those described in Galatians 5:19-21. For one to be usable in the hands of God, he needs to put away his old nature and be renewed in the inner man.

> *Most of us are endowed with gifts which are lying dormant and can only come out when we are exposed to the wilderness.*

Another reason why one goes through the wilderness is to be enlightened and educated of one's potential and to harness it for the purpose of the ministry. David realized much of his potential through his experience in the wilderness. Moses's training in the wilderness enhanced his leadership ability. Most of us are endowed with gifts which are lying dormant and can only come out when we are exposed to the wilderness. For some of us, God takes us to places where we are left alone to experience things which teach us our capabilities. For all you know, your skills will be perfected and refined as you go through the lessons of the wilderness. David's strength came to light when he was faced with challenges in the wilderness, and that was why Goliath was no match for him. The wilderness is therefore a good period to develop your gifts effectively, because those gifts will be an instrument to bring to pass God's purposes for you and your generation.

Key things to note about the wilderness:

- ➢ The wilderness is God's training ground for His army and generals. Training and preparation are required and essential – if you fail to train, you fail to win as well. You are likely to be ill prepared and will fail to meet the target set for you. Most people believe that training is not essential, but the essence of it is to learn of techniques and common mistakes that can be avoided. Skillful as we may be, coaching is essential to our success, hence the training.

- ➢ We all have our Egypt in us. Egypt represents our past lives in the world before we came to know God. It is the place that reminds us of our slavery and departure from God. No matter how sweet our Egypt may appear, it is not the place God has destined us to be. Sometimes we think of the leisure and the pleasure of Egypt, and become satisfied with it and begin to see it as the Promised Land. But God in His wisdom is taking us to the land purposed for us. He will have to empty us of the baggage that comes with us from Egypt in order to fill us anew with His glory and power for outward demonstration.

- ➢ As heirs to the throne, we cannot claim our legitimacy as we continue to stay in someone else's country and operate as a ruler. The president of the United States cannot live and claim to be president if he is not a U.S. citizen; that is a basic requirement. The Prince of Wales cannot exercise his sonship and rulership over the people of another country, but rather only where his powers and authority are accepted. Similarly, as children of God, we cannot claim this heritage as we dwell in a land that is not of our Father. He therefore creates the opportunity for us to live out of our past – Egypt – in order to make us partakers of the Promised Land – Canaan – flowing with milk and honey. Before we get to the promised land, be it ministry or whatever God has planned for us, we need to go through our wilderness.

➢ God's purpose for the wilderness is to train possessors of visions and take them to their promised land. It is one thing to realize the vision for our generation, and another thing to achieve that vision. You cannot claim to have the cure for diseases such as HIV/AIDS or tuberculosis, without testing and proving it.

➢ The wilderness is a place of skill development and empowerment. Without wilderness training, there would never be empowerment. For some of us, we desire to be used by God, but fail to pay the price for qualification into God's army. God's power is strong and eminent to bear witness that we are His messengers. The word of God is a tool for liberation of the soul and a way of securing eternal life. His demonstration of miracles through the hand of Moses in Egypt and the catapult in the hands of David is enough to take the world and the enemy by surprise. The regular army is given skill training in combative and defensive mechanisms. In the same way, God is enrolling us for training in His army to have the skills necessary for battle. Joseph's skill of interpreting dreams was better shaped in Egypt through the things he went through. David's skill of playing the harp and singing was developed when he was a shepherd boy. He used to entertain himself, not knowing that the King would one day need that skill. What you know how to do best is what God polishes during your wilderness training as a tool for His deliverance and salvation.

> *No one decides to go to the wilderness, but it's the Lord Himself who takes His children to the place to train and equip them with His signs and wonders.*

> *It is a must for all believers to go through the wilderness process. Sometimes we may not understand why we go through certain experiences in life, but they are God's intended purpose in order to complete in us His will.*

➢ No one decides to go to the wilderness, but it's the Lord Himself who takes His children to the place to train and equip them with His signs and wonders. But it must be emphasized that, *it is a must for all believers to go through the wilderness process. Sometimes we may not understand why we go through certain experiences in life, but they are God's intended purpose in order to complete in us His will.* What is left then is to understand what they are meant for, and make those lessons available for the next person. What you have now is deliverance and opportunity. Some of us may not know and understand why we go through certain challenges in life, but sometimes it is hidden until we come to the stage of maturity when God perfects His will in us.

➢ The Lord decided for the Israelites to pass through the wilderness in order to train their hands for war. Coming from slavery and its mentality, there was a need to change their minds and attitude to be able to own their possessions. They were going to live among people who would fight them. With no known experience of war, having a spirit of fear and timidity, they were going to give up; but as God wanted to make them a mighty nation, they went through the wilderness in order to learn the act of war. We as 21st Century Generals should understand that we are engaged in both spiritual and physical warfare, and the wilderness training is necessary for us to qualify for God's end time army. (Ephesians 6:12) Being equipped will teach us the strategies to disarm the devil and his agents.

➤ The wilderness embodies what God does. He empties us of what may hinder us for the task and equips us with what He needs us to have to complete the task. The world out there is a war zone. The prince of the world, Satan, is the ruler. Our mission is to reach out to the world for the Lord. My understanding of military intelligence is that you cannot be successful if you underrate the might of your opponent. Years back, the United States of America failed in Cambodia because they ignored this fact, but that informed them of how to make future advances towards other countries in terms of war. The Lord trains and teaches us the strategies of war to outwit the prince of the world and to make us effective in His kingdom.

➤ God needs us to be intelligent over the smartness of the devil. We are not to be ignorant of him (2 Corinthians 2:11), and that is why God trains us. A wilderness experience causes us to depend on God for our daily bread and sustenance. Although we may need to plan for the future, our spirit is taught to receive manna from Heaven on daily basis. It was important to God to show the people that He is Jehovah Jireh – God the provider. We work so hard sometimes but earn so little – not only in terms of finances but also in terms of realizing our dreams – all because we fail to depend on God and trust in our own understanding. *"Trust in the Lord with all your heart and lean not on your own understanding. In all your ways, acknowledge Him and He will direct your path."*(Proverbs 3:5-6)

Lessons from the Wilderness

> *The wilderness teaches us to develop absolute trust in God and not to be self-reliant or put our trust in man.*

➢ **The wilderness teaches us to develop absolute trust in God and not to be self-reliant or put our trust in man.** God brings people to a point where there's nothing we can do to save our own life. He does it so we will continue to depend on Him. In the supply of quails during the wilderness walk of the Israelites, God told them to take only what they would eat that day and the next. That is why in the Lord's Prayer, Jesus taught us to ask God to "give us each day our daily bread." Planning for the future is necessary as children of God. Our plans for the future must be anchored on the word and direction of God. As seen in the life of Noah, he built the ark for 120 years in anticipation of the flood as he received the word from God. We sometimes toil, crave, and work our whole life for material things, and leave the world without fulfilling God's purpose for us. We spend our whole life toiling for things that may not be eternal. Depending on God daily during our time in the wilderness helps to build trust in Him and ushers us into His purpose and will for our lives.

> *Depending on God daily during our time in the wilderness helps to build trust in Him and ushers us into His purpose and will for our lives.*

➤ The wilderness is a place where God makes a covenant with us as well as generations to come. He gave the people of Israel the laws and the commandments in the wilderness through Moses. In our wilderness, God gives us the opportunity to know more of His dealings with us and establish His covenant with us and the generations to come.

➤ When God ordains, He sustains.

➤ The wilderness affords us the opportunity to defeat the giants and enter our promised land.

CHAPTER TWO

Joseph's Wilderness Experience

• •

Some are born as agents of change. Others come on the scene to continue what has been started, whilst many do not know why they are in life.

• •

P eople who do not know their purpose live a routine life and just want to please themselves. But then there are people like Joseph, whose life brought change for many generations to come. Such men form the catalyst for God's agenda and assignment for their families, cities, nations, continents, and generations. *They have the spiritual insight and tenacity to see beyond the now and to allow themselves to be agents of change.* They endure the shame and the trials of life because they are aware of what is to come. Joseph's change came at the age of thirty years old. He was someone who could interpret dreams with certainty. Perhaps it was a bitter or a mixed experience, but he was a young dynamic visionary and a prophet of his days. Joe, as I may affectionately call him, was a truthful and an honest gentleman. For his honesty, he was hated and persecuted by his brethren. We live in a world where you are applauded for being evil and "smart" rather than speaking the truth.

Rejection and Denial

Joseph had unending tales of unverified lies leveled against him by his own brothers. I once had a pictorial image of how Joseph felt at the age of seventeen, a young undergraduate with prospects to earn wages and pursue other ambitions in his life. Such a brilliant guy was ideal for his master's and/or doctorate degrees in the not-so-distant future. But his life dreams and goals came to an end when he was forcefully taken as a slave and sold by his own brothers. He felt rejected and then betrayed; he had feelings of hurt and unforgiveness. The seed of evil could have been sown in him. He could have shot and killed his brothers and been sent to court for murder. His rich daddy could have hired him a brilliant lawyer to defend him. But he sat in prison in Egypt, serving a sentence for crimes he did not commit. What must have happened to his dreams?

How was he going know if he would ever be able to marry or not? To have children, and grandchildren? Life seemed to have come to an end!! But, then he remembered that change is inevitable. According to Job 14:14, *"If a man dies, can he live again, No. All the days of my appointed time will I wait till my change comes."* And that was how his wilderness experience started.

A Beloved Son Becomes A Slave

"Now Israel loved Joseph more than all his children, because he was the son of his old age: and he made him a coat of many colours. And it came to pass, when Joseph was come unto his brethren, that they stripped Joseph out of his coat, his coat of many colours that was on him."(Genesis 37:3)

When Joseph was caught, put in a pit, and sold to the Ishmaelites, God looked on him, just as He did on his own Son, Jesus Christ, on the cross. And it was all for the purpose of bringing to pass His sovereign Will and counsel in their lives. As a child of God, never think that God is not interested and concerned about your situation. He may have something better ahead for you.

Dear reader, you may be enclosed in your prison of thoughts. What and where you want to see yourself may be far-fetched. You might have received many prophetic words which appear not to be materializing. Such was the feeling of Joseph in his early days. Sometimes, we question God about how and why the righteous experience leads to failures and misfortunes in life. God has not called us to disgrace, but to perfect His will in our lives. (Jeremiah 29:11).

God's training requires us to know His ways, not his acts. At times it is difficult to reconcile the current position with the future promise. It is said that what you will become tomorrow depends on the decisions you make today. As much as I agree with this, I also think that everything is subject to change, as set out in Ecclesiastes 9:11: *"I returned, and saw under the sun, that the race is not to the swift, nor the battle to the strong, neither yet bread to the wise, nor yet riches to men of understanding, nor yet favour to men of skill; but time and chance happeneth to them all."*

For with God, what is not known to us is more than what we know. Who could have predicted the end of Joseph – sold into slavery, tried for rape, sentenced to imprisonment? Who would have thought of him becoming a leader and second in command in Pharaoh's government as well? Our trust in God and desire to live right and faithful before Him is the surety of our future on this earth and the world to come.

Forgotten as A Reward

"And the chief butler told his dream to Joseph, and said to him, 'In my dream, behold, a vine was before me;' ... And Joseph said unto him, 'This is the interpretation of it: The three branches are three days: Yet within three days shall Pharaoh lift up thine head, and restore thee unto thy place: and thou shalt deliver Pharaoh's cup into his hand, after the former manner when thou wast his butler. But think on me when it shall be well with thee, and shew kindness, I pray thee, unto me, and make mention of me unto Pharaoh, and bring me out of this house.'" (Genesis 40:9-14)

There seemed to be some hope for Joseph at the age of twenty-eight when he interpreted the dream for the chief butler as indicated in Genesis 40:14. The forgetfulness of the man he had helped could not take away his faith in God. It took another two years for him to realize the dreams of his teens, thus it was thirteen solid years before realizing the vision. He was composed and hoped for the fulfillment of the vision. ***When everybody seems to have forgotten about you, remember that God never forgets His child.***

"And it came to pass from the time that he had made him overseer in his house, and over all that he had, that the Lord blessed the Egyptian's house for Joseph's sake; and the blessing of the Lord was upon all that he had in the house, and in the field." (Genesis 39:5)

What good have you done that you think you have not been rewarded for? Man sometimes forgets about others when the situation is not about them, or when their condition becomes better – but God doesn't!

Don't make the mistake of taking your reward from man. He can only help and save you when he feels more secure, and the tendency to forget it all is high. Many times, man's focus is on himself, but we are God's focus. He is more concerned about you than anything else.

"For I know the thoughts that I think toward you, saith the Lord, thoughts of peace, and not of evil, to give you an expected end." Jeremiah 29:11

We may at times be accused of things we have not done. Joseph's episode is typical of such situations. Look at Job's accusations by his friends regarding his misfortunes. They believed he was suffering because of his sins. (Job 8:1-5)

The depth of your sorrows and trials will determine the height of God's placement in your life. The lower you sink, the higher your rewards!

What have you gone through that makes you think God is not there? Have you been rejected, criticized, disqualified, or discredited before? These men of wilderness experiences all went through these moments and periods. They were honest and faithful, and yet still experienced adversities. Understand that God uses those periods to work and perfect His will in our life. As a child of God, you must be convinced that all these things work together for your good.

"And we know that all things work together for good to them that love God, to them who are called according to his purpose." (Romans 8:28)

Lessons from Joseph's wilderness experiences:

➤ He *forgave* his brothers for the pain they made him go through, hence the name Manasseh for his first son. Forgiveness is a divine act. Though difficult to practice, it is a well of healing to the inner man and the soul. We all get offended in one way or the other, and we offend others as well. If you cannot forgive others when they wrong you, you will also not be forgiven when you wrong others and even God. In Jesus's teaching on prayer in Matthew

6:12, He taught us to pray for God to forgive us our sins as we forgive those who sin against us. Forgiveness is not an option or something we can negotiate, but is essential for our service to God.

➤ As a man of vision, he *focused* on the end result rather than the suffering for a season. (Hebrew 11:26) He learned how to be abased, but still to abound and enjoy life. He endured all that with the hope of fulfilling the vision.

➤ He *hoped* against hope. He was futuristically inclined. He then sacrificed and suffered in order to help fulfill the prophecies and the promise of God. He was available for God to use. Many of us are sometimes **able**, but not **available**, for God to use.

➤ In all the things he went through, Joseph continued to *sharpen his skills* for the future and to do good things. He was a dreamer, and not only did he remain one, but rather developed it to the extent of interpreting dreams. ***Progressive development is a tool for realizing your potential.*** He worked on his potential, talents, and gifts. This calls for burning extra hours to improve and develop yourself. Take classes relating to your field. Seek counsel from mature people in your discipline. Just make the effort to add value to yourself. Continuous improvement will shape you for your future work.

➤ He had a *heart of service* and was endowed with the skill of planning (a strategist). He took delight in offering his services to whoever needed him, irrespective of their lineage and status; he was an impartial, loyal, and committed fellow. No wonder God promoted him in His own time. A heart of service brings us blessings and favor.

➤ He *remembered* where he was coming from and where he was going. He told Pharaoh about his people. He did not change his citizenry status even when he was made a prime minister. Sometimes we do certain things for acceptance rather than living to please God.

➤ Joseph was a prophet who *spoke into the future* of the generation to come. He spoke of the prophetic leaving of the people of Israel from Egypt. He was a man of God with the spiritual insight and foresight for the future.

Joseph was not a known preacher. He was neither an evangelist nor a called prophet. But he functioned in his position and demonstrated God in his life. He did not change his faith in God because he was in a foreign land. He did not wait to be called into full-time ministry to hate and run away from evil.

The time is now, whether you are a nurse, teacher, politician, pastor, student, engineer… you are called to demonstrate godliness and affect your generation for the better. The 21st

Century Generals are men and women showing forth God's glory in their offices, schools, marketplaces, hospitals, and churches for God to save His people. Joseph's experience was captured more in prison and a foreign land; he held on to the faith and continued to demonstrate his belief in God and to live for Him. Sometimes we tend to have different lifestyles, depending on where we find ourselves. Our profession of Christ is only known when we are in the midst of church folks, but not the nonbelievers. It is difficult to know the difference between a non-Christian and a Christian today if he doesn't say it. But Joseph lived beyond reproach in his life and continued to sanctify God and demonstrate Him wherever he went.

When he became a prime minister, he continued in his faith, never refusing to identify with his people and serving God and mankind with the experiences gained over time. A man's worth is his contribution to others and society at large and not the accumulation of wealth. Archbishop Duncan Williams of Action Faith, Spintex, Accra Ghana once said, **"A man is not successful until his success reflects in the lives of others."**

Though the distance between the dreams Joseph had and the materialization of them was long, he hoped against hope for the fulfillment of them. He positioned himself to fit into God's deliverance agenda for his generation. He served his generation with a sense of purpose. No wonder, in the sharing of the lands among the twelve sons of Israel,

Joseph had a double portion of inheritance through his sons, Ephraim and Manasseh.

God will always reward your faithfulness, no matter how long it may take to serve Him.

Some Useful Lessons to Note from Joseph's Life

The Pride of his Dreams

I believe that Joseph was the type who boasted of his future to his brethren because of his ability to see what was to come, which was the envy of the rest of the family. It would have been impossible to think that all ten brothers rose up against him. Yes, he had the ability, but his delivery was wrong. I have met many people in life who have great potential and skill, but are destroyed by their way of talking or speech and attitude. The presentation of thoughts, ideas, and conversation should win admirers for ourselves rather than enemies. You can read more in Dale Carnegie's book on how to develop confidence in the act of public speaking and how to make and win friends. The problem may not be the dream he had, but the presentation. Sometimes we have difficulties because of our attitude. It may either be with our bosses, colleagues, or family members. Wherever that challenge may come from, we need to examine ourselves and avoid strife where possible. Remember that your gift may take you to a place, but your character/attitude will retain you there. According to Brian Tracy, intelligence is a way of acting. If you act intelligently you are smart, regardless of your IQ.

The Strategy B Factor

Until you speak it, no one knows what is inside of you except God. Sometimes we talk too wild and too loose and expose ourselves to unnecessary spiritual attacks. The enemy got to know that deliverance was near for the Israelites and tried to kill Moses. Immediately after Herod heard of the birth of Jesus, he sought to kill him as well. That confirms why you need to guard your dreams and visions and not talk too loosely about them. Some of the people we share with in the spirit of friendship sometimes turn against us in many ways. This must have been one of the weaknesses of Joseph, telling his dreams all the time.

We must be guided spiritually as to who we share our dreams and visions with. It is not ideal to go about telling everybody about your plans. Learn to write them down and pray over them and be led to share with the right people. Especially when it comes to open and personal prophecies, pray over them until they have manifested, rather than relaxing and talking all the time. I learned this lesson in a painful way. Sometimes, we suffer due to our own inability to use Strategy B, and that is: keep the vision and dream, pray on it, and choose carefully who you share with. Remember, any time you speak, you are on trial.

21st Century Joseph

Joseph represented the love of his father. He was gifted with potential even at a tender age. He had a dream of greatness – like you can envisage for yourself now – but was confronted with the wickedness of his own brothers. His experience and suffering at the hands of his own brothers brought pain to him. He became bitter and shattered. But his wilderness experience represented an act of forgiveness. After going through it, he became *better,* instead of being *bitter*, and forgave his brothers.

"And Joseph said unto his brethren, 'Come near to me, I pray you.' And they came near. And he said, 'I am Joseph your brother, whom ye sold into Egypt. Now therefore be not grieved, nor angry with yourselves, that ye sold me hither: for God did send me before you to preserve life.'" (Genesis 45:4-5)

We live in a world that makes people hurt us, and we also hurt others. Sometimes it happens from people we least expect, and that makes us bitter. You can become bitter when you realize that your mother wanted to abandon you at birth or your father did not accept your mother's pregnancy. We become so embittered and unforgiving, and that brings so much pain and affects our relationships with others as well. Since this is not outward, we grieve and groan within. As 21st Century Generals, we ought to come to a place of forgiveness for our church members, family members, and those who have hurt us badly. I can recall a friend whose father told him that his (the friend's) mother tried to exchange him for a girl because she needed a girl;

this hurt him a lot. It affected his relationship with others, especially his mother, and his performance in life generally. Once when praying with him, the Lord spoke to me about it, and after sharing, we prayed for a healing process. May the Lord grant you the grace to become better and forgiving like Joseph did. One way to deal with it is to forgive yourself and others. It is difficult, but rewarding. I have learned to do it, and each day is a new lesson, a new experience of learning how to be forgiven and forgive others as well.

CHAPTER THREE

Moses in the Wilderness

. . . .

Wherever God is taking you TO, you need to go through this experience in order to get there.

. . . .

Moses also had a nice wilderness experience. His experience is a mixture of God's desire for His men and women of the 21st century. Moses was known as a personal friend of God, the only man who probably saw God in his natural state. He experienced all the miracles that one can think of. As we examine his experience, let us also learn a lot from him. This is the man God used to give the law to the people of Israel.

His life was divided into three periods. The first forty years, during which he lived in Egypt was a time to know and learn the ways of the people. He was privileged to live in the palace by divine act, and also as part of God's agenda to save his people since it was time for a change. He lived in Egypt, but did not allow Egypt to blur his focus. He still identified himself with his people.

"Choosing rather to suffer affliction with the people of God, than to enjoy the pleasures of sin for a season." (Hebrews 11:25)

But I must say that, during this period of training, he had the best of educations. The favor of God in his life from his birth paved the way for him to have the best of the land and not to experience the suffering that the Israelites were going through. However, he made the choice to suffer with them. If we can fulfill the purposes of God for our lives and our generation, then it is time to make the right choices and forgo the comforts of sin and its pleasures.

The life of Moses for the first forty years was initially successful, but more or less a failure to him at the end. He could have given up after he was sought for high treason and murder. But God had a plan for him, and the first inevitable thing happened to him when the Lord took him to the wilderness to learn of the terrain. He learned the act of leadership in the palace as a prince in the kingdom of Egypt. It was God's design for him to be born into the palace. Your place of birth is your palace, but this does not matter as much as the impact you create for your generation. Unknown to Moses, the Lord was preparing him for a task. As a trained Egyptian, he did not lose sight of the sufferings of his people. He sought to be a deliverer by killing someone and adjudicating a matter, but God used that opportunity to take him to the next stage. It is good to know what God wants you to do than to do what you possibly think God should do.

Though God's timing for the deliverance of His people was not yet up, He was nonetheless working through Moses about his task for the future to bring deliverance to those who rejected him. Moses had passion for his calling. What are you passionate about? But the statement stands that "the stone that the builders rejected became the cornerstone." A preacher man once said, "When the timing of God for your life is due, the very people who once asked 'Who are you?' are the same people who will say 'How are you, Boss?'" Timing makes the difference. Moses's passion for his people's deliverance made him a fugitive until the right time came.

Little did he know that sojourning in the wilderness of the Midianites was part of God's plan for him. This would be the second phase of his life. Sometimes God allows certain things to happen to us in order to complete His will in our lives. Moses's qualification as someone to lead the people from Egypt was done in the wilderness. The work of learning how to survive in the wilderness because of bullies and to fight and encourage the people were all done in the forty years of his life in the wilderness. Though blessed with a wife and a child and resources, he learned to obey God when the time was due. One thing I love about him was the constant contact he had with his family members. At the time of his calling, his brother Aaron was about to meet him. But listen, when the vacancy for a deliverer was announced, Moses was so qualified for the job because he had all the working experience. His weakness as a stutterer was not a limitation to what God was preparing him for. Whatever you are going through will give you an experience of some sort, and God will surely make a path for that potential. **I want to emphasize that the working of our skills during wilderness training is very much essential and calls for discipline to develop it.** It is these skills and gifts that will make room for you. No condition is permanent. *God is not dealing with you for nothing.You are who you are today because of His plans for your future.* (Jeremiah 29:11)

Moses's heart was still close to God, and he had not forgotten the traditions of the patriarchs – Abraham, Isaac, and Jacob. He might have heard and read of them, and he gratefully kept contact with the God of the fathers. He had a heart of service, and God used this to show Himself to him. At the age of eighty, Moses was appointed as the commissioner for delivering Israel from Egypt, a great and a challenging task. But he was so experienced, although he did not know from the beginning that God had justified him for the job. Not only was he to deliver them from Egypt, but was also to take them to the Promised Land shown to the patriarchs.

So, Moses became a deliverer and a possessor; that was his third phase. But was he able to achieve all he set out to do? As we examine these qualities in him, let us also understand that he could not finish his task.

Reading the book entitled *God's Generals* written by Roberts Liardon, you learn of men and women used by God, and how some were not able to finish the task given to them. When the Lord told me that He was taking me through the wilderness experience, He first taught me to know and understand the strengths and weaknesses of his people and gave me the caution to learn and take Him at His word.

It was a period of hard times because I experienced much rejection and neglect from people I was confident of receiving attention from. Sometimes I was so down in my spirit that I thought it was not worth serving God. In the midst of prophecies and promises, I could not fathom the way forward for life. But hey, I went ahead to learn, read, and experience a lot, and I'm forever grateful to God for what He is still teaching me. That has made me develop a conviction of doing what God wants me to do each day of my life, rather than what others think that God wants me to do.

I remember when I became a student and an associate pastor in a church. I loved the people, and doing the work of God at that time was my delight and desire. But God said, "Son, the time for ministry is not now, and you have not finished yet what I want you to know." I was told to leave the church to go and learn other things. My skill of writing was polished thereafter because of some experiences I went through and the people I met in my life. Although it was right to have remained a pastor at the time, it gave me another opportunity to know more about God's dealing with me which cannot be discounted.

We sometimes graduate when God has not graduated us. I heard about one man of God testifying that He went into ministry work more than ten years before he was called by God. After twelve years in ministry, one day the Lord said to him, "Son, I have now called you to serve me." As I listened to his testimony, I asked myself, *What was he doing all this time? And what should he have done that he didn't do?*

Moses's lessons were not known by him – when God was going to call him and what he was doing in his life – but his experience was enough to make him the right candidate for the job.

> *For some of us, the guilt of our past still haunts us and prevents us from forgiving ourselves. But when we are saved, God, through the blood of Jesus forgives us and wipes away the sentences and the wages of sin.*

Moses's objection of not being eloquent enough to speak was the guilt he had for going back to Egypt. He thought that the death sentence was still pending against him. And God needed to assure him that all the people seeking his life were dead. For some of us, the guilt of our past still haunts us and prevents us from forgiving ourselves. But when we are saved, God, through the blood of Jesus forgives us and wipes away the sentences and the wages of sin.

First, the acceptance of Christ as our Lord and Savior translates us from death into eternal life. (John 3:36) Again, God, through this act, blots out every ordinance and sentence that bring accusation on us. He orders the removal of the cloth of stain and puts on us a new dress made of white. The significance of the white dress is His righteousness that He gives us. (Galatians 2:20)

We are therefore justified to proclaim our liberty to the world. We as 21st Century Generals should come clean before the world so that they may not point accusing fingers at us. Jesus said, *"The prince of this world is coming, but he has nothing in me."* (John 14:30)

Lessons From Moses's Weakness:

The Passion as a Deliverer

Early in Moses's life, when he started going out from the palace to visit the people, he experienced fighting among people which he thought he could handle on his own. His attempt to kill the Egyptian was what he thought was justice for the suffering of the people. His thoughts were right, but the idea and approach was wrong. Killing the Egyptian was not the solution to the deliverance of the people of God. We should match good intentions with right and honest acts to please God. Hence, he was not willing to stand trial for his own action and inaction. Instead, he fled. What makes you run away from others at your workplace, church, school, or place of abode?

Moses was quick-tempered, and this affected his ministry greatly. Imagine staying on the mountaintop for forty days, fasting to receive the commandments, only to come down and throw it away and destroy it because of the people's disobedience which God had already told him of.

The devil always seeks out our weaknesses and continues to use them against us. It is one of the means he uses to drain our anointing and to expose us to the ridicule of the world. **If you fail to control what dominates you, you become captive to it. Watch out! Always be on your guard.**

Anger

Anger is a necessary evil, but it can lead to a destructive end. Moses was quick-tempered. Instances in his life and how he handled those issues confirm that. For instance, the casting down of the Ten Commandments was as a result of his anger and the pressure he felt for leading the people. We ought to be conscious of people around us, and must not allow their mistakes to cause us to exhibit the wrong attitude. This trait can really destroy your good plans and purposes. We must learn to deal with it, rather than take the approach that it is something we cannot overcome. Your own issue may be pride, moral weakness, stealing from others; whatever it is, if you fail to control it, it will prevent you from fulfilling God's purpose for your life. For this same anger, when he was told to stretch the rod, Moses hit the rock with the rod. He could not reach the Promised Land because of this simple act. As insignificant as this act may seem, we should note that God required absolute obedience!

"Take the rod, and gather thou the assembly together, thou, and Aaron thy brother, and speak ye unto the rock before their eyes; and it shall give forth his water, and thou shalt bring forth to them

water out of the rock: so thou shalt give the congregation and their beasts drink. And Moses took the rod from before the Lord, as he commanded him. And Moses and Aaron gathered the congregation together before the rock, and he said unto them, 'Hear now, ye rebels; must we fetch you water out of this rock?' And Moses lifted up his hand, and with his rod he smote the rock twice: and the water came out abundantly, and the congregation drank, and their beasts also. And the Lord spake unto Moses and Aaron, 'Because ye believed me not, to sanctify me in the eyes of the children of Israel, therefore ye shall not bring this congregation into the land which I have given them.'" (Numbers 20:8-12)

Miracles cannot take us to Heaven. They are God's evidence to the unbelieving world. They are not extraordinary with God. Despite all the miracles performed by Moses including the mountain experience, the devil had the gall to contend for his body, according to Jude verse 19. In Matthew 7:22-23, Jesus rightly put it to those who claim to have used his name to do miracles: *"Depart from me, for I do not know you."* What is needed is character to sustain us in the area of our calling in life.

Moses of the 21st Century

Our time will lead us to witness many who do not know why they went through certain experiences in life. They were placed at the location by God to fulfill His divine agenda. Some of us may be released as deliverers for our family to save them from what we call "family reproach." Others have to endure hardship because of the divine assignment on their life. What is important is to identify your passion in life and discover God's purpose for it. Never under-utilize your potential. When the opportunity comes your way, acquire all the training you need. Never allow your past failures to intimidate you; confront them and move on to fulfill the tasks before you.

The Moseses of the 21st century are men and women God is counting on to deliver generations to their Promised Land. His power is not limited, but rather strong enough to break down the defenses of the Pharaohs of our days. They are men and women who are not limited by their resources, age, and time, but know what their God can do. Men and women who can give to God what is in their hands for Him to use. Just like Caleb, age is not a factor. Men and women who know where they come from and identify themselves with the people just as Moses did. Records have it that the first five books of the Bible were written by Moses.

God is raising Moseses who will be sensitive to the burning bush experience and respond to the call, not those who will lose focus because of the comfort they find themselves in. With God on our side, we should seek to reach our Promised Land. Though Moses failed, he prepared his generation for the Lord, as read in the book of Deuteronomy. These are men and women who have the next generation in mind and can prepare them to take over from them. Moses prepared Joshua by training him. When you are no longer here, who will continue the good work you started? Any time you become jittery of your successor, it must question your leadership skills. **A good leader is not the one**

who can do it all, but rather the one who can have many others to do it just like him. Such was the life of Jesus. Three and a half years of effective ministry left a generation who continued the vision to our days. We have the baton now, and must be prepared to hand it over right.

> *A good leader is not the one who can do it all, but rather the one who can have many others to do it just like him.*

Lessons from Moses's Experiences:

Timing

"There is a season for everything, and a time for every event under heaven." (Ecclesiastes 3:1)

It is always important to identify our timing concerning our events or actions. While leaving comfortably in the palace, Moses clearly understood his mission on Earth as a deliverer for the suffering Israelites but found it difficult to understand the timing. Many of us, like Moses, are aware of what God wants to do with our lives, but lack the basic timing of it. Any premature act before the right time may not bring the desired results, no matter how good the intentions may be. And when we delay too much, we also will miss the target. Moses killed the Egyptian at the wrong time and hence had to flee. We should always ask the Holy Spirit to help us to identify the right time. **Remember, God is never too late, nor too early, but always**

right on time to fulfill His plan. Moses's life teaches us this useful lesson that we must also look to. Check out this scripture about Jesus: "He began to say to them, 'Today this Scripture has been fulfilled, as you've heard it read aloud.'" (Luke 4:21) There is a right time for God to fulfill His purpose in you, and it does not matter how long it takes.

> *Remember, God is never too late, nor too early, but always right on time to fulfill His plan.*

Passion and Compassion

Whatever you have passion for can come out one day, be it good or bad. Passion distinguishes the real from the many. Compassion is the commitment that empowers us to follow our passion and work it out. Moses had passion for the people of Israel, and it was no surprise that God used him to deliver them. One of the pieces of evidence in the ministry of Jesus Christ was the passion He had for the people who always followed with compassion. He loved to do things for them; God granted that desire. This lesson would enable us to check and understand ourselves better. Whatever you become passionate about can define your history. Let us therefore know what we must work on with passion, and be motivated to achieve it.

CHAPTER FOUR

The Israelites – God's People through the Wilderness

. . . .

Let God use you to reach the world!

. . . .

A typical wilderness experience was seen in the lives of the people of Israel. God decided that for them to reach the Promised Land, He had to take them through the desert (wilderness) to train, test, and refine them to possess the land. Though the journey could have been for only forty days, it took forty years to complete.

- ➤ They were God's own people, chosen out of the generations in the world. (I Peter 2:9)

- ➤ God made a covenant with Abraham, Isaac, and Jacob to be their God and to make Israel his people. (Psalm 105:9-10)

- ➤ By His divine purpose, He took them into Egypt through Joseph to prosper them and to show Himself strong on their behalf. This was part of the calling and choosing of Abraham to fulfill his prophetic agenda for mankind. (Psalm 105:15-21)

➤ He walked with them on the prophetic word that He would give them the Promised Land after completing a service in Egypt. (Psalm 105:37)

➤ They were easily noticeable because of the favor of God in their lives that brought them increased blessings. (Psalm 105:43-44)

All of these things happened to them because of God's desired purpose for them. At the heart of this was the desire to train them as possessors of the Promised Land shown to Abraham 400 years before. Whatever happened to them was not by chance, but rather according to God's perfect design. **To you as a child of God, things don't just happen to you by chance – they are planned.** So when the years had passed, He raised a man to deliver them from oppression and slavery in Egypt.

His arm was strong on their behalf, and performed so many miracles to aid their suffering, which included the killing of every firstborn son in Egypt. By God's mighty power, he wrought miracles and signs for them. Many more of such examples can be found in the book of Exodus in the Bible.

To fulfill His purpose, He decided to take them through the wilderness for the following reasons:

➢ to empty the mentality of slavery in them

➢ to show them that He is the God of their fathers and they are His people

➢ to train their hands for war

➢ to test their level of faith and commitment to Him

➢ to make them possessors of the promise – the land flowing with milk and honey

➢ to advertise them to the nations

➢ to teach them how to depend on Him daily for sustenance

Let us deal with the issues that confronted them, according to 1 Corinthians 10:1-9.

As I studied the lives of the people from then to now, I have come to terms with the prophecy that they hold the key to God's agenda on Planet Earth. They have experienced both angelic and divine visitation. They ate of the heavenly food (manna), were baptized in the Red Sea, justified by faith to possess the land, and yet they failed to reach this target. These were some of their failures and the things that did not please God. Remember, what they went through was meant as a lesson to us.

Lessons of the Wilderness Experience: (1 Corinthians 10:1-22)

➤ They murmured against God. Murmuring in this case was a bitter complaint about the ability and capability of God. They doubted His words! How do *you* treat the Word of God?

➤ They tested Him. Again and again, they failed to believe His miracles and were always desirous to go back to their old life of slavery (Egypt). They thought the past was better than the now. But to God, our now is always the best for us. It has been said that: *"Yesterday is a history, tomorrow is a mystery, but the now is a gift – that is why it's called the present."*

➤ They chose other gods beside Him to worship. A god is anything you adore and worship more than your Creator, God Almighty. Our success, wealth, education, work, and others can be a god to us. Anything that occupies the first place in our lives apart from God is to be watched. They failed because they were idolaters. What is first in your life? What do you love most?

➤ The Israelites failed in the walk of faith and exhibited a carnal lifestyle and attitudes towards spiritual things. They insistently and consistently desired Egypt as a better place to where God was taking them, though they had not seen the good of the land. What God intends for us is always better than what we see as good for us. I am reminded of when Abraham asked Lot to choose a place for them to separate for peace to prevail. The Scripture says: "*And Lot lifted up his eyes, and beheld all the plain of Jordan, that it was well watered everywhere, before the Lord destroyed Sodom and Gomorrah, even as the garden of the Lord, like the land of Egypt, as thou comest unto Zoar. Then Lot chose him all the plain of Jordan; and Lot journeyed east: and they separated themselves the one from the other.*" (Genesis 13:10-11)

What Lot thought was good brought him many troubles. He lost all his possessions and his wife when God destroyed Sodom and Gomorrah.

Do not be deceived by outward appearances; God knows better than we do. The saying is true, "All that glitters is not gold." Do not settle for aluminum; your wilderness experience with God will refine you to have your gold. The filthy and unwanted sand mixed with gold ore when processed by fire sifts out the impurities and brings out the precious mineral of gold desired by all and worn by royalty. I can see your unrefined moments that include your wilderness moments, but I also see your refined days when you will come out as a tested instrument in the hands of God to fulfill His assignments. (Psalm 105:17-19)

➢ They doubted Him, and worst of all, sinned against Him. They were to live a life of faith and believe God would take them there. They lived in the carnal world and could not perceive God's agenda for them. God was disappointed about their faithless life. The Bible says, *"The just shall live by faith."* (Romans 1:17) How often are we able to live this Scripture in our lives, especially concerning our family, career, vision, ministry, and marriage, among others? This, the Israelites failed to do, and by that sinned against God. **"A faithless life is a sinful life."**

➢ Some of them fornicated against Him, and in a day, 23,000 people died. We can ask ourselves, *How can we commit such sin?* For many of us, we have become addicted to filthy films and pornography as they roll on our computers, phones, and television. We have no standards for the type of programs we watch on TV. We play, sing, and remember worldly songs that do not bring us spiritual upliftment, instead of building our most holy faith with spiritual hymns and songs. (Ephesians 5:19) These actions, among others, constitute obscenity and provocation against God. They are equal to fornication in its strictest sense. That is, anything that takes away the place of God's holiness in our life constitutes fornication against Him. God actually needs our unflinching support and loyalty.

But in this generation lived men like Joshua, Eleazar the Priest, and Caleb, who unlike many others who died in the wilderness, became partakers of the promise. How do we relate to God when we are going through difficult times? Do we sometimes murmur, insinuate, and doubt if God is there? We question why all things go wrong, and ask if He is interested in our business. I have, and on many occasions felt just as human as the rest of us. I cannot justify this, but ought to learn from God what He is teaching me.

The experience of these people is worth considering. They actually experienced miracles, signs, and wonders. And yet some failed to please God, whilst others did please Him. We ought to understand that the significance of their lessons to us in the present is that: *"Many are called, but few will be chosen."* (Matthew 20:16)

Signs and wonders don't make God; they only give us a sense of proof of His existence. We need to go beyond that in order to trust, believe, and obey Him. We need to be careful about our ways and amend our lives. We should not view the Israelites as failures and sinners, but learn of their examples so as not to fall victim to the same things that tempted them. (1 Corinthians 10:10)

The 21st Century Israelites

We have an opportunity to be known as and called God's children. The Israelites were God's chosen people with the purpose of reaching the Promised Land and establishing God's covenant with Him. They were made aware of their wilderness experience from day one when God sent Moses to them. One would have expected that, having a defined assignment, they would have focused on it and pleased God; but yet they did the most abhorrent things against God.

We, the stock of the 21st century, have a great responsibility to learn the lessons they left us with. Apostle Paul stressed in 1 Corinthians 10, that we ought to watch the things that made them displease God. As we become aware of our calling, ministries, and divine assignments, we must endeavor to fulfill them and not become disappointments and failures. The shocking story of the Israelites' wilderness experience is that, of the many people who started the journey, only two were privileged enough to go to the Promised Land. Again, we need to bear in mind the saying of our Lord Jesus Christ that *"many are called but few will be chosen."* Being called is an opportunity, but will you be part of the final selection? We need to remind ourselves that the starting is as equally important as the finishing, and it is much better when we finish because rewards are given there.

Twenty-first century Israelites must keep focus, fight against any distractions, and move forward to reach our Promised Land.

In his book, *Maximized Manhood – A Guide to Family Survival*, Dr. Edwin Louis Cole wrote, "The biblical Israelites failed to live in Canaan by faith for God to fulfill His promises to them. To us now, the just must live by faith and anything short of this is a failure. God's promises can be fulfilled in us and through us if we learn to approach Him in faith."

Lessons from the Israelites:

Faith

The Israelites' wilderness experience was a test of faith and a belief in God. It is true that many of them failed this test; yet, they demonstrated their commitment to the God of their fathers. By faith and through the workings of God's miracles, they left Egypt for the Promised Land. One useful lesson from them is that our faith should be exercised daily in order to please God. It is not a one-off act that must be abandoned once used. The Christian walk is an act of faith, and the just must certainly live by it. It is useful not only to have a promise and a prophecy like the Israelites, but also to see it come to pass. The test to see it come to pass as some of them did is to count God as faithful to fulfill what He has said He will do. Hebrews 11 teaches us the legends of faith, and we must be encouraged to live it in our days to manifest God's purposes for our lives.

"For the just shall live by faith." (Romans 1:17, Hebrews 10:38) Our daily walk must be based on this faith. A Christian life without an exercise of faith will never reach its Promised Land. A faithful Christian life is a continuous daily living and walk with God.

The Winning Mentality

The lessons from Joshua and Caleb, who were among those who took the journey from Egypt to the Promised Land, give us insight into a winning attitude. In spite of the challenges and the dangers the journey, they were looking to the end result rather than what was confronting them in their present. The end result was that God promised them a land and a place of rest, and they believed He would do this in spite of the giants they saw. This attitude made their God bigger than the problem, and they believed Him until they possessed the promise. Even at age eighty-five and beyond, they were fit and strong for battle and able to conquer. (Joshua 14:10) To succeed in this life, we must have a winning attitude toward God and trust His word that once He has said it, He will surely do it with us.

CHAPTER FIVE

David and his Wilderness

· ·

*"We should never know the music of the harp
if the strings were left untouched; nor enjoy
the juice of the grape if it were not trodden in
the winepress; nor discover the sweet perfume
of cinnamon if it were not pressed and beaten;
nor feel the warmth of fire if the coals were
not utterly consumed"-Charles H. Spurgeon*

· ·

Dave, as I may affectionately call him, was a man after God's own heart and a generational changer. As a child, his desire was to love, serve and worship God. God found him to be the perfect substitute for the King of Israel, since He knew he would teach the people the ways of the Lord. (1 Samuel 13:14). A multi-faceted young man, he served as a shepherd for the family, developed his mastery and bravery by interacting with wild animals in the course of his work, as well as developing his potential in the music industry. Little wonder he wrote many songs and left us with lessons about what he went through. His life experiences are worth noting because of the lessons they give us. He also made a lot of mistakes that affected his family and his later reign in Israel, but God kept his promise in His days. David's wilderness experience is relevant to our days (1 Samuel 26:2). All that he went through and the lessons thereof are recorded in scriptures so that the prudent will learn and avoid them. Many a time, I hear people saying, "even David did this." For instance, they argue that even David married more than one woman. The lessons of all these acts of David are recorded in the Bible so that we can avoid the acrimony, hurt and rivalry it brings to siblings and the family at large.

David, a shepherd boy at an early age, was raised by God as a man after God's own heart to be the second king of Israel. David's life purpose was to manifest the prophetic declaration of Jacob regarding blessing his children, as revealed concerning Judah in Genesis 49:8-11.

"The scepter shall not depart from Judah, nor a lawgiver from between his

feet, until Shiloh shall come: and to him shall be the gathering of the people."(Genesis 49:10)

Until David came on the scene, this word had not manifested. All the other tribes produced judges and leaders except the mighty Judah house. David was therefore a generational changer who, through his dedication, service and calling allowed himself to manifest the agenda for posterity.

Lessons from David's Wilderness Experience

Reading about David's life brings out the following lessons of wilderness preparation:

Training and Skills Development

➤ He had no known laurels to show, in order to be given an opportunity like that.

> *"And Saul said to David, Thou art not able to go against this Philistine to fight with him: for thou art but a youth, and he a man of war from his youth."*(1 Samuel 17:33)

As far as King Saul was concerned, David was not qualified to fight and definitely not against a giant, but his skills and training were enough to open the door. Hence before God he was qualified to fight. **"God doesn't call the qualified, He qualifies the called." (1 Corinthians 1:27-29)**

➤ At times we feel we have enough in us to take responsibility, but the system says you need to justify yourself before being considered and sometimes you have no experience to show. *A good friend and a big brother, Ato Robertson says "there is always a first time in everybody's life and that should form the basis for the next line of action. No one knows what is in you unless you show what you can do by your experience."* The world looks for standards but

God qualifies us with His standard when we are called by Him.

➢ David's wilderness training developed his confidence in God. His statement that "the God who delivered me from the hand of the bears and wild animals" was enough to show how He trusted and believed God would allow him to kill the giant. He could match his wilderness experience with the challenge confronting him. A good student is the one who can use the lessons learnt in the classroom to answer problematic questions in examination as well as in real life situations. *The tough times have only one solution; our ability to recall and trust God for the next move.*

➢ He made use of what he had and had worked with and not something superfluous. It's usually better to be yourself, not just a copy of another person. The world we live in is full of imitation because people fail to be innovators. The world is deprived of its richness because bearers of great visions of churches and business are living as copies not originals. David was comfortable with what he had. That brought him success and not the armory of Israel. Saul and the other armies had the weapons but could not kill Goliath. In fact, David would have needed a great deal of training to use his new apparatus, but it was easier to make use of what he has tested before. **"Go in this thy might,"** the angel told Gideon. (Judges 6:14) We need to believe in what we have and convince ourselves of our ability and capability to do what is required of us. *Be yourself. Never be anybody else apart from you.*

➤ His skill of playing the harp also made room for him in the palace. *Don't underrate what you have today because someone may need it tomorrow.* The Lord always creates the need for your skill. Proverbs 18:16 says, *"A man's gift makes room for him, and bringeth him before great men."* The Lord made room for David just as he did in the life of Joseph. Whatever your skill and your potential may be, *develop it and don't discard it.* The time will come for it to be exercised. Here I may refer to both your spiritual and physical potential. *Potential is one's ability that becomes useful for others to benefit from.*

➤ He continued to practice daily in order to improve himself. Upgrading is the word. *You cannot go up unless you learn to climb the ladder.* There is no end to the search for knowledge in this world.

"And further, by these, my son, be admonished: of making many books there is no end." (Ecclesiastes 12:12a)

➤ Take the course you desire to take. Pursue that dream and practice on a consistent basis. Remember, it takes many hours of training but few hours for the show. Lack of preparation will render you unqualified for the job. For some of us, it is not because we are not capable, but rather rusty. If we fail to deliver when the opportunity comes, we may likely not have the chance again.

David's personal qualities included the following:

➤ He was handsome and ruddy. This is how God crowns us with His favor.

➤ He was a skillful player of harps and a talented musician. He had a potential, and so has each one of us.

➤ He was a mighty and valiant man, a potential commander of the army. He knew how to behave himself in the house of Saul. We are God's army and must therefore have discipline. *"For we fight not against flesh and blood but against principalities, powers of darkness, spiritual wickedness."* (Ephesians 6:10)

➤ He was prudent and wise in handling matters. No wonder his son became the wisest man who ever lived. In his book *Secrets of the Richest Man Who Ever Lived*, Mike Murdock shared the experience of Solomon's wisdom. Reading the books of Proverbs and Ecclesiastes confirms the wisdom of Solomon.

➤ He was a comely person and a man of war. He knew how to formulate strategies and move ahead. He was a strategist. The world we live in now needs men and women of such skills and gifts. God is the source of all great strategies.

➤ He was a man who feared God. His reverence for God brought him favor before men, especially the king at the time called Saul. (Luke 2:52)

➤ He was respectful and obedient to those above him. People who normally don't want to serve desire to be leaders and expect total submission from their subordinates. This is not right. What you want others to do for you, do unto others.

➤ He had good anticipation and foresight of his timing and knew when things were ripe. He operated with a spirit of insight and understanding.

➤ He was courteous and behaved wisely. He respected protocol and gave honor to whom honor was due. What we go through in life is sometimes reciprocal and comes back to us. Jesus put it this way: "*Do unto others what you will want them to do to you.*" (Matthew 7:12)

➤ He did not bother himself about the victories he had had in the desert, for he was certain that the glory would come someday. No wonder when the women sang about his destroying 'tens of thousands' whilst Saul was commended for having killed a thousand, it meant nothing to him. Many of us demand recognition and acceptance before men. We force our way out to catch the eyes of our superiors. But scripture says promotion and honor comes from above. (Proverbs) *David's unaccounted victories in the desert were recognized. He killed only Goliath but they sang of his killing tens of thousands. The unrecognized victories in the wilderness were all added to his current one.* Life has its own timing with regards to rewards, according to God's plan. Don't give up when no one knows what you are doing. Your Heavenly Father sees it and will reward you someday.

➤ God made the army of Israel helpless in order to bring to the stage His wilderness trainee. He created that inadequacy to project the adequate training given to this shepherd boy in the wilderness. God will always create in you the desire to fulfill a purpose when the need arises. My exhortation to you is to take your training seriously and endure the wilderness whilst you learn your lessons, because the day will certainly come for God to lift you up. In such times, the scriptures in Romans 9:16 will be fulfilled: "*It is not him that wills, nor him that runs but the Lord that shows mercy.*" David was not part of the regular army, let alone captain of the troops. It may sound absurd to us to have a guy with no military background become the army commander and lead troops against an enemy. *But God had prepared him, justified him, approved of him and what was left was the acceptance of man. When God is through with you, man will have no option than to accept you*. Their lessons are parallel to what we may encounter in life.

Lessons from his Weakness:

➤ David trusted himself so much and because he was considered to be ruddy and handsome, he married many women. His polygamous life led to infighting among his children during his life and even after his death. The acrimony, infighting, the killings and the rebellion of his children attest to this fact. We must learn to be humble in what God has blessed us with and/or enables us to have. Whatever position you attain in life, if there be any praise and something to boast of, do it in the Lord. (Philippians 4:8). This is what David failed to do. He mistook God's grace as his personal achievement and did what he was not permitted to do.

➤ He married many women and had many concubines and bore many children when he felt that God has established him and given him rest from his enemies. At certain times, we come to a point in our lives of academic, social, financial and political success and we believe that it is a license to do whatever we like, but we should always remember that, to every action and decisions that we take, there are consequences and repercussions for us to bear. God remains the same and his foundation stands sure. (2 Timothy 2:19)

David of the 21st Century

In our days, God is raising men and women with skills and talents and unseen experiences who have developed their trust and confidence in God. These people believe in His possibilities to take nations and kingdoms for God; they are men and women with the mandate to manifest the prophecies concerning their families and nations. There exists in our days, giants of all forms in businesses, families, nations and continents as well as many other areas of life. There are still scary giants like Goliath with established systems and extensive experience in traditions of culture and attitude who believe that theirs is the only way. But in such cases, it is not the act of war we should pursue, but our ability to recall our encounter with God and to bring that experience to the place of our birth. I see a generation embedded with the experience of David (1 Samuel 17:35-37) to take away the reproach and shame on our families, nations and continents. God is raising people who can put an end to situations that conflict with and confront their belief and faith in God and can cut the head off these Goliaths and bring victory to their generation.

Dealing with the big brother syndrome is a challenge to us. In our pursuit of our goals and dreams, the majority of us face a "big brother" that puts us down just as David's big brother did. (1 Samuel 17:28). His shortsightedness made him see David as haughty, but God's timing was near.

We need to remember the times of men such as Martin Luther King Jnr. who defied the conditions of black slavery in America and give birth to the civil rights movement that paved the way for equal rights for black and white. Whilst David was seeing the victory because he had been through the wilderness and knew that God's time was to come, Eliab, the big brother was focused on the individual. Whilst David had a major assignment to become a leader of Israel in the future, Eliab thought he was to take care of a "few sheep." When you fail to define your goals in life, others may spell it wrong for you. In such cases, blame no one but yourself.

A common test of our vision should always be to look at what benefits it will bring to others rather than to us. What change will come if I take this course or direction? How will my society, nation, and/or family benefit from it? Whenever the answer is, when you trust in God, He will give you the strength to tear down the walls of apathy, defeat, and reproach. In such instances, we should resist whatever pressure there is, defy the odds and obey the voice of God to bring about the needed change.

David's wilderness victories, though not known by anyone at the time, were summed up after killing Goliath.

CHAPTER SIX

Daniel's Wilderness Experience

· ·

"Gilt is afraid of fire, but gold is not: the paste gem dreads to be touched by the diamond, but the true jewel fears no test"- Charles. H Spurgeon

· ·

Daniel's experience was had in slavery. He went through the period in captivity. For most of us, this would have been an opportunity for us to deny God and live carefree lives. Daniel was born in the days of the captivity of Israel. I have come to realize that it is not where you come from and the conditions in which you find yourself but rather God's help that makes the difference. According to John Johnson, one of America's best motivational speakers, *"Men and women are limited not by the place of their birth, nor by the color of their skin, but by the size of their hope."* After all, Jesus was born in a manger and yet he was the Savior of the world.

Daniel, in a strange land, still stood for God. Many people who were once on fire for the Lord in their local

61

communities travel to foreign countries and forget all about the church and the things they use to do. They just backslide and think that life must go on without God. Others simply forget about God when their conditions change for the better. The 21st Century Generals must learn not to do this from our honorable brother.

Daniel's Wilderness Lessons:

In captivity, Daniel still proved his faith in the God of his fathers and gave us these lessons:

Captivity, Challenges, Compromises and Change

He lived in the days when it was easy for people to compromise with evil. Doing so was a command from the King, the ruler of the Earth at the time. After all, the Bible even says that God instituted leaders and so we must obey them. Despite this, Daniel did not sin against his God. A faithful and blameless young man was born and taken into slavery. It would have been easy to deny God because he was suffering for a sin he did not commit. Obeying the King's command to worship his imagery was to submit to those in authority, and someone could conveniently hide behind a scripture to do so. Sometimes we are tempted to accept doing what is not acceptable to God because of our fear of our superiors.

We compromise for a pittance by doing all sorts of things with the belief that "God will understand." The Jews at the time knew that they could have or serve no other god except Jehovah God, but the pressure and the demand of the times was enough for them to accept the command of King Nebucadnezzer.

We are challenged as young people to have boyfriends and girlfriends because everybody is doing it. We go all lengths in our businesses and offices to do things which are not right, just because it has become the order of the day. Arguably, we sometimes support our vice with a scripture in order to give credence to its practice. A Christian who wants to justify his drinking habit may say that the Bible actually does not condemn it and even the apostle Paul asked Timothy to drink a little. According to the Book of Proverbs, wisdom will teach you how to know what is right, good and fair.

Daring to be different was what Daniel and his three friends sought to do. Nowadays, we are pressured as preachers to speak what the people want to hear rather than what the Lord is saying. Is it possible that, as in the days of the prophet Micaiah, the lying spirit – which is a spirit of compromise – is working in our midst? (1 Kings 22:19-23)

Politicians compromise just to win votes and have the numbers. We hardly consider morality and true convictions from God. Choose to do the right thing and you are branded and tagged as "old fashioned." Therefore, for fear of being isolated, we compromise like any other person just to be accepted. Look at schools, private lives, workplaces, market centers and even the church and you will understand that there are no differences. I said in one of my writings, that *the church has become worldly as the world has also become churchy.* Twenty-first Century Generals need to be defiant and kick against the spirit of compromise.

One truth of all these men was their absolute trust and belief in God. Talk about Moses, Joseph, David, Daniel and Jesus himself and you will understand that they feared the Lord. Fear of the Lord means to depart from evil and do that which is right and of sound doctrine. (Proverbs 8:13). If we can move the world to God in our generation, then we need to demonstrate the fear of God in our lives as an example for others to follow. We should not only talk about it but practise it. Better put, *we should not talk the talk but rather walk the walk.*

> *If we can move the world to God in our generation, then we need to demonstrate the fear of God in our lives as an example for others to follow.*

Some of the characteristics of Daniel worth considering include the following:

➢ He believed in God. (Chapter 6:23) He desired God's approach to situations rather than using his own intelligence.

➢ He had his spiritual and moral values right.

➤ He stood for principles and did not compromise on his beliefs.

➤ He had wisdom and was a learned fellow. We as 21st Century Generals should not be ignorant but rather accept all opportunities for learning as they come our way. Both secular and informal education is needed as part of our information wealth in order to deal with the world around us. (Daniel 1:17)

➤ He worked on his skill – the act of interpreting dreams. He had an understanding of the times and in due time God made way for his skill.

➤ He was resolute and bold enough to speak the truth without fear or favor. He stood for honesty and his principles.

➤ He was a man of prayer and even prayed when it was the law for all the people of the land not to pray to any other God, except the god of the king. (Daniel 6:10) Prayer was his way of life.

➤ He was a man of fasting and could read the times. He combined the virtues of Christianity and did not leave out the basics of life.

➤ He had an excellent spirit. You could hardly find fault with him. He walked perfectly before all men and God. Apart from what others might have considered as his controversial stance on religion and faith, he was revered among his contemporaries.

➢ He could not stand pretenders and hypocrites. We become sycophants trying to sing the praises of men in order to earn our daily bread. But as men of the 21st century, tempted by evil and many vices, we need to let our **yes** be **YES** and **no** be **NO** and stand for the truth no matter the cost.

Daniel of the 21st Century

A new breed of politicians must emerge in our days. The Daniels of the 21st century must be men and women of honesty, integrity and with the fear of God to eschew evil – *people who will not change their godly principles for political and positional expediencies.* For a very long time, politics has been a dirty game. But Daniel was an administrator and a prince in the kingdom of Babylon as well as in Mede and Persia who stood for principles, lived for them and triumphed over the forces of conspiracy that arose against him. His faith in God, honesty, trust and submission to the rulers of the times, along with a fear of God was proof of God in his life. He was the only one who served in leadership positions in different empires under at least three great kings. His excellent spirit made room for him before all men.

The 21st Century Daniel represents men and women of insight, knowledge, wisdom and understanding. Insight is the ability to gain an understanding of situations and appreciate the ways of dealing with a situation. It can be said to mean having an advance knowledge of a situation. From the Greek word "phronēsis" *(fron'-ay-sis);* it means mental action or activity; prudence, wisdom.

Knowledge on the other hand is the accumulation of information. To be knowledgeable means to be informed of an activity or to be instructed in a discipline.

Wisdom therefore is the application of knowledge in order to obtain better results. According to the Book of Proverbs, wisdom is better than riches. Proverb 16:16 says, *"How much better is it to get wisdom than gold, to choose understanding rather than silver!"*

Revelation is having insight into what happened many years back without you knowing of it, and having the future shown to you, along with having an understanding of how to handle it.

Daniel's insight into the times and seasons gave him access to a revelation of the times we live in. Daniel was transported into our era to see what would happen in the end times. His gifts of interpretation and purposefulness made him an intercessor for the deliverance of the people from slavery. As men and women of this age and era, God is beckoning us to be available in order to make known his unsearchable truth of what is happening in our marriages, homes, social and secular lives and to reveal what is to come.

We need to sharpen our insight and understanding to discern the times we live in and to overcome the temptations that confront us. We need to show the spirit of excellence in our duties as fathers, husbands, politicians and whatever we do in this generation. There was nothing that they could accuse Daniel of. When our accusers bring their accusations, is there merit to what they are saying? May God give you the kind of insight He gave to Daniel and his friends so that we can serve our generation with all sincerity.

The fact that the world accepts something does not necessarily mean God approves. All the other princes accepted the King's command to bow to his idol but Daniel and his three friends refused. Can we have men of integrity in our political circles whose interest is to serve the people, rather than themselves and their cronies. We have to be men and women who will settle for God's best and nothing less, not men who will be morally bankrupt and academically or professionally good. We shall all give an account of our lives to God. Our success must be holistic and without question in our academic, social, marital and every other area of life.

CHAPTER SEVEN

Jesus's Wilderness experience

. . . .

Without trials, there will be no triumph.

. . . .

The Son of God's experience

There were prophecies about Jesus's birth just like Samson and some others in the scriptures. His birth was surrounded with the fulfillment of these prophecies. The news of His birth was broken to the shepherds and the world during the census of King Augustus. But from just after His birth to the age of twelve, not much was heard of him. He lived in quietness, learning and preparing for his appointed days. The Son of God also went through life stages to fulfill His work of sharing the word of God with us.

> *I believe that a man's mission in life defines his vision.*

When his preparation was complete, Jesus appeared on the scene to fulfill His mission. *I believe that a man's mission in life defines his vision.* We cannot live for everything.

Our lives should have a sense of purpose about why we are here on Earth and what we ought to do. In the book *The Purpose Driven Life*, Rick Warren attempts to answer the questions that every man and woman on Earth must ask in order to live a fulfilled life. According to him, we are not created by accident but rather for a unique assignment on earth such as to Know God, Grow in God by developing relationship, serving God and sharing Him with others through God's Love and Honouring God by worshiping Him. Thus, our purpose in life must be defined by these principles.

Jesus's Wilderness Lessons

Jesus's wilderness experience can be summed up as the forty days of fasting and prayer He had before the beginning of his Earthly ministry. Almost all the gospel writers recorded this particular incidence because of its significance to our walk with God. The lessons in the forty-day fast and the eventual overcoming of it formed the solid foundation of Jesus's work. The stages of temptation He went through with the devil is typical of the things we go through in life as we desire to do the work of God. These can be summed up in His wilderness training. But He learnt to master and deal with the following. Our study will reflect on the Gospel of Luke chapter 4:1-14; a typical wilderness incident.

➤ He fulfilled and confirmed what we ought to deal with in order to be useable by God. A classic example is the passage from the gospels. In Luke 4:1, Jesus fulfilled the first act of righteousness of being baptized and was led into the wilderness to be tempted. The journey of our wilderness begins when we accept Christ as our Lord and Savior.

➤ His first temptation was to turn stone into bread – "showmanship." He learnt how to appropriate the gift of God. The abuse of God's power should also be looked at. When the devil asked Him to turn stone into bread, what he meant was for Him to be a show boy. It was easy for the Son of God to perform that miracle. Remember, He fed five thousand people with only five loaves of bread and two fish and gathered twelve baskets more from what remained. The miracles performed by Moses were just the manipulation of the rod in his hand. But what do we do when we have power? Power, whether religious or secular must be exercised with God's discretion. Jesus learnt how to appropriate the power He received and not to dissipate His anointing on any unnecessary act as a matter of showing off. The use of God's gift must not be exploited for material and personal gain, but rather used for edification of the body of Christ and to the glory of God.

➤ Jesus learned to conquer these things which pose a great challenge to us.

➤ He learnt the word of God and used scripture as a defense against the devil. He made his reference point in defeating him, *"For it is written…"* Some of us are more familiar with our pastor's and bishop's words than the word of God. But any word that is not the word of God and the scriptures should be ignored, no matter who said it. As 21st Century Generals, we must be students of God's word.

"Study to show yourself approved unto God, as a workman who needs not to be ashamed but able to divide rightly the word of truth." (2 Timothy 2:15)

➤ He had control over the lust of the eyes. *A preacher man once said, the heart is the eye of our spirit as the natural eyes are to the body.* What we see naturally has an effect on us. For most of us, our desires are stirred up by what we see with our naked eyes. The devil showed Jesus this but He was able to deal with the lust of the eye and overcame it. If we are to be effective in our generation, then we should not pretend not to be seeing but rather learn the art of dealing with the lust of the eyes. The power of sight can be used positively to achieve greater things for God. Today's fashion and media are all filled with the filth of evil to blur our sight. Even adverts for food often come with nudity of some sort just to entice us.

➤ Jesus took pride of life and desired to have a part in it. There is nothing wrong with being blessed. Rev Eastwood Anaba (one of the charismatic preachers in Ghana) once said, *"God poured his riches and we were fortunate to be at the position of receiving and that is not a crime."* But ask yourself this; what do you boast about? Is it material possessions, education, fame and popularity among others? Which of these things can save us from God's judgement? *It is not of work that any man should boast.*

"For by grace are ye saved, through faith; and that not of yourselves: it is the gift of God: Not by works, lest any man should boast." (Ephesians 2:8-9)

➤ *"Pride is the seed for destruction."* (Proverbs 16:18) Some of us need to watch out for the seed of pride that can easily mar the beauty of what God intends to do in our lives. We should not be boastful of what we can do but rather thank God for His gift. This is what Jesus did.

The quest for popularity and fame at the expense of virtue should be looked at. Jesus's wilderness experience revealed that He could have received the title from the prince of this world, but remember Jesus was not of this world. *Who you are and what God has for you as a package is better and greater than whatever you may receive in exchange from the devil. Do not give your Christ for a pittance!* Many of us have empty titles! Life is not about titles but results. What benefit is a title when it cannot be used to produce tangible and positive results? How can society benefit from a medical doctor who has never practiced?

> *Who you are and what God has for you as a package is better and greater than whatever you may receive in exchange from the devil.*

Learning to overcome the temptations of life marks the beginning of our obedience in fulfilling God's desire in our lives.

The craze for popularity and riches drives people to do all sorts of things. We kill, cheat, lie and falsely accuse others in order to satisfy the greed in us. The devil presented this side of life to Jesus and asked Him to worship him for them. Understand that whenever your motivation and your focus becomes "getting it all, no matter what," then you have to watch out.

The devil is not as ignorant as we perceive him to be. In fact, he must have learned lessons from his previous dealings with mankind. He knows when to appear as a light angel to cloud our thinking, but an in-depth knowledge of the word of God will make us smarter than him and will expose his ways and equip us to deal with his extensive experience.

In Luke 4:5; the high mountains showed him the kingdoms of the world:

> ➤ Dealing with the lust of the world; the craving and greed for all things.

➤ Dealing with the desire for power and recognition

➤ Dealing with enticement and lack of discernment

➤ Setting the right priorities with regards to worship. Worship is for God and anyone that receive it apart from the godhead opens himself up to destruction. (Acts 12:22-23)

➤ Identifying deception and dealing with the truth rather than what seems to be a fact. Truth is not relative but rather a certainty. God alone is to be worshipped.

➤ Going for the gold. Why settle for what the devil gives knowing well that God will give you the best if you endure the testing moments?

The Holy City

The city is a place of attractions and potential diversions. Sometimes we are confronted with fantasies rather than reality. Dealing with the Holy City includes the following:

➤ The Pharisee spirit – the spirit of religiosity. Our world is full of people who know about Christ and God but live a life outside Him. It is more fashionable to belong to a religious sect rather than be a Christian. If the world is filled with the 10% of the Christian community quoted, then we should be able to turn the world to God. But there is so much pretense that we have to deal with.

➢ Dealing with pretense and hypocrisy.

➢ Departed strength and spirit, e.g. Samson

➢ Dealing with the worst enemy – pride

➢ Not taking things for granted. A sin is a sin no matter how it is defined.

➢ Arming yourself with information and using it at the right time.

➢ Determining the right moment to act.

Willpower

Life is full of decisions and choices. A choice is based on action or inaction. The prayer of Jesus in Luke 22:42 introduces the types of willpower that we have: the perfect will of God and the will of the evil one. Man as creation is a recipient of the two through the kind of choices we make.

The Perfect Will of God

This is seen as the predestined plan of God for mankind, and as such, every human being who arrives on Planet Earth. The debate as to whether it can be altered or not is purely subject to the decisions and the choices we make. God said to Jeremiah that He knew him, named him and called him for a purpose and that before he was conceived in his mother's womb, He had plans for him. (Jeremiah 1:5) This shows His perfect will for us. God is interested in every detail of our lives, including knowing the number of hairs of our head. He has named us and called us into this world to fulfill a task.

But how many of us are able to achieve His will? I sometimes cannot marry the true prophetic word of God concerning an individual with his present state. As I was wondering why some people are not able to achieve such purposes, I came to realize that, certain times, we fail to play our part in bringing to pass God's agenda in our lives, thereby nullifying the materialization/manifestation of His purposes.

The Will of God

Jesus prayed saying, *"Father, if thou be willing, remove this cup from me: nevertheless not my will, but thine, be done."* (Luke 22:42)

Do we sometimes ask God for His will in our lives before we make decisions? If we accept that God is interested in everything about us, then we will need to find out his will for our schooling, our place of living, our marriage and all other things.

In Proverbs 19:21; the Bible says, *"There are many plans in a man's heart; nevertheless the counsel of the Lord, that shall stand."*

A plan is an intent of action to be taken and how to go about it. But a purpose is the original intent of the maker and its use. For example, the potter has an intent and use for the pot he creates. This explains God's intent for you. He therefore will bring to pass as you desire, pray, obey and walk in it to bring to pass His purposes for your life. Jesus's prayer was not to change the original plan of God for His life but to allow it to come to pass. No matter how difficult it may be, if we can understand it and know His will, we will overcome the challenges it may pose to us. We will be able to endure the test of the times and follow the example of Christ, as in Hebrews 12:2:

"Looking unto Jesus the author and finisher of our faith; who for the joy that was set before him endured the cross, despising the shame, and is set down at the right hand of the throne of God."

Jesus as Our Example

Joseph was a type of Christ in his days; thankfully he was able to endure his wilderness training. Moses as the lawgiver is another typology of Christ, as Christ is the giver of grace to us in this dispensation. The Israelites were to overcome the wilderness challenges but they failed. Most of the failures of the Israelites in their wilderness experience were overcome by Christ to show us that it is possible. David as a shepherd boy reflects Christ as the chief shepherd. (John 10:11) Daniel, a blameless man of prayer is another classic example of Christ in his generation.

Joseph is a topography of Christ in the Old Testament. Just as he was loved by his father, so is Jesus the begotten son of God. (John 3:16) Both were hated for their good work. Joseph was sold to a foreign country, as Jesus was sold by Judas Iscariot. (Genesis 37:26; Matthew 26:14) Joseph felt dejection from family, friends and trusted people as Jesus himself was betrayed by the people he had fed and nurtured. (Mark 15:9-15) At death, they were both deserted. They took away Joseph's clothes as Jesus's clothes were taken and a lot cast on them. (Genesis 37:23) They plotted to kill Joseph as they plotted to kill Jesus (Genesis

37:18-20). Joseph was sold to the Islamites for twenty pieces of silver whilst Jesus was sold for thirty pieces of silver by Judas Iscariot. (Matthew 26:15) But the end result of it all was God's preparation towards their elevation. I have wondered why God sometimes refuses to talk to us when we are distressed and in pain and as we recall the prophecies and promises, they seem to be too distant for us to reach them. We pray all manner of prayers, pay tithes, fast and do whatever we can possibly do for God's attention but His sovereignty determines what should happen to us according to His purposes in our lives. God looked upon Joseph when he was caught, put in a pit and sold to the Ishmaelites just as He did to his son on the cross. All for the purpose of bringing to pass His sovereign will and counsel in their lives. As a child of God, never think that God is not interested or concerned about your situation. He may have something better ahead for you.

The Israelites too mirrored Jesus in the Old Testament. By God's agenda, they went to Egypt but not all of them came back to the Promised Land. For even Moses the deliverer failed to get to the land God told him to take the people to. But Jesus was sent to Egypt and came back preserved as a child. Pharaoh sought to destroy the Israelites just as Herod sought to kill Jesus. According to the scriptures, Egypt is the place where God preserved the elect in times of difficulty, but it is not the final destination for His people in His plans. For instance, the entire family of Jacob was preserved and saved during the famine in Egypt through Joseph. (Acts 7:14-15) Moses was preserved in Pharaoh's house during the time of the killing of all male children. (Exodus 2:1-10) Jesus, our Savior, was taken to Egypt for preservation from the hands of the jealous Herod who heard of the birth of the King of the Jews. (Matthew 2:13-15) Even David, during his wilderness moments and trying times fled to the land of the Philistines to save himself from being killed by King Saul. (1 Samuel 27:1) Therefore God always chooses a place to secure us in order to bring us to his perfect place – the Promised Land.

Jesus of the 21ST Century

Jesus Christ, according to the scriptures *"is the same yesterday, today and forever, Amen."* (Hebrews 13:8). It is therefore important that, as His followers, we live a life of Christ here and now and wherever we find ourselves. He is the salt of the world and therefore we must provide taste and preservation for a tasteless world. He is the light of the world and so we must shine in the darkness around us and provide comfort through Christ. He is the hope of our salvation and must be a better example of His hope in the hopeless world.

He lived to overcome sin and the challenges of life, and we must also overcome sin by His seed in us. The Bible says that he that is born of God will overcome sin. Since Christ conquered sin, He gave us the power and the ability to also overcome the power of sin and live a holy life in service of God. That is why we are a holy nation and a royal priesthood of God. (1 Peter 2:9)

When the world is looking for Christ in our days, we must be the perfect example of Christ to them. We must come to the place where Paul said anyone can look up to him to follow his example because he has imitated Christ. Jesus Christ should be honored through our lives by the example we live among men. Remember, He is still alive through us and we must show Him forth.

CHAPTER EIGHT

My Wilderness

. . . .

Many people are born to this Earth but few make history either by their positive or negative actions. Your experience is a platform for making an impact and leaving a footprint for others to follow.

. . . .

At certain times, learning lessons the hard way may be a bitter experience and a mistake that could have been avoided if we had listened and learnt from other people. The movement of God in our time will only achieve the desired results if we critically examine the lessons in the movement to avoid common mistakes. As I lay down one day, reflecting on my life, the Spirit of God told me to make my experience available to my generation. That is why I'm sharing my betrayals, failures, success, achievements and lessons. The love of God is stronger than any other professed love without the fear of God. We should appreciate and show this towards our neighbors.

In September 1996, when I had just finished my polytechnic training, the Lord asked me to come before Him to pray. I went to the prayer ground not knowing what to expect.

I didn't find the reason for being there until the third day when the Spirit of God said to me, "Son I'm going to teach you the success and the failures of my great men and women and will cause you to learn them so that you can share with others." He showed me and taught me to learn and take His word at a go, since failure to do so would result in incurring His displeasure. The example of Balaam the prophet was given to me. He taught me of King Josiah as the greatest of all the people and explained that what man considers a success is usually different from how He sees success. That began my wilderness experience. This material is a compilation of the lessons learnt over a ten-year period. It formed the foundation of my ministry. Some of the things that He said to me happened to my amazement, and sometimes I am awed by the occurrences because they happened with **foreknowledge.**

The Zeal for Christian Ministry

Christian ministry has been my desire ever since I got to know and understand my mission in life. One day God told me who gave me my name and shared His purpose for my life. He revealed His plans for me and told me that He had not spared me challenges from infancy in every area of life that you can think of. From childhood experiences, through schooling, work and marriage, and many more areas in my life, I have fought battles like any other person. For instance, I have always had issues with my examinations one way or the other. From junior high school to sixth-form, the Polytechnic and University, it happened either in the form of sickness, missing examination results, a missing certificate and many others.

Your life is important to God. The moment you accept Christ as your Lord and Savior, God unfolds His will in your life, and the devil will fight it to prove a point. Indeed everything is possible and that is why you also need to stand and defy the odds and believe in God to come out victorious.

I was not spared challenges during my adolescence. I grew up in one of the "hotspot" suburbs in Ghana and, being exposed to all forms of vices and influences, it took the grace of God and strict discipline from my parents to bring me up in the fear of the Lord. Peer pressure was also a great factor. My father maintained a strict godly discipline that was combined with Mom's prayer of intervention to help us overcome the teenage years. I remember an incident that led to some form of giving up on my behavior, but thank God for the prayers of my mother, I was strangely led to the grounds of the Resurrection Power Ministries in Santasi, Kumasi in 1987 and that marked the turning point in my life.

The Migration Era

Life is in stages and the knowledge of the word of God takes us through each stage. When I finished my university program, I was sent back to work in Kumasi for my company in a different capacity. I was then actively involved in youth work in Accra and did not want to move at that time, since I was enjoying it. The conditions I gave to God were satisfied when He brought in a brother to the department to continue my work there. Many of my friends did not understand why I had to move on, but *one thing I have learnt is to do what God wants and not what I feel.* Had I followed what I felt only, I wouldn't have made certain decisions. But following what God wants gave me the opportunity to continue unfinished work in the city again and, by the grace of God, we were able to build a youth organization that is still doing well, even in our absence. God used that period to affect the life of another generation.

I came into contact with different people who influenced me and shaped my life in one form or another. I had the opportunity to publish my first book and do other things for God.

Marriage

Marriage also taught me some lessons of life. I do not try to justify myself in this instance but rather to say that God is faithful. I did not expect the challenges I had to go through in my marriage because of my background of serving God from my infancy. I thought I deserved more since I had always lived a "pious life." But God used my marriage to deal with my pride of righteousness as well as make my lessons available for others and to heal their wounds. My latter encounter with others and the opportunity to counsel them through my experience attest to this fact. One of the greatest challenges I faced during this period was my inability to forgive myself. And, as most of us do, I kept asking God "why me" instead of asking "what do you want me to know?". *It is a fact that God does uses you to bring about a change.* We enjoy reading the story of Joseph and Job, forgetting that they went through those moments to teach us now the lessons of life.

Whatever happens to us in life is not the finality of the situation, but rather our attitude towards it that will determine the outcome. What you are going through or will go through is not meant to kill you, but to strengthen you. Learn to forgive yourself and move on in order to know God's next move for your life. Even if you have made a mistake, make a genuine turn to God and ask Him to show you His next move for your life. Like Job in the scriptures, most of us rather turn to complaining and condemning ourselves instead of looking for the solution to the situation. When God came to Job, He told him to stop condemning himself but rather look to Him for direction.

What you may need to do first of all is forgive yourself, forgive those who might have wronged you in the process, and begin to pray for them. Then you will see the glory of God manifesting in your life. Jesus said, *"Father, forgive them because they don't know what they are doing."* (Luke 23:34)

If you were Stephen being stoned, would you have made this prayer in Acts 7:58-60?

"And cast him out of the city, and stoned him: and the witnesses laid down their clothes at a young man's feet, whose name was Saul. And they stoned Stephen, calling upon God, and saying, 'Lord

Jesus, receive my spirit.' And he kneeled down, and cried with a loud voice, 'Lord, lay not this sin to their charge.' And when he had said this, he fell asleep."

But this led to the salvation of Saul who became the great apostle Paul. Learn to release the pain in your heart towards those who have wronged you and let go. Be it a colleague at work who has wronged you, a boss, a family member, a spouse, a parent or a child, a pastor or a church member learn to forgive yourself and the person as well. When we are not able to forgive ourselves, we cannot forgive others. Whatever pain it has cost you, let go.

Sometime back in deliverance ministry, I realized that some of the causes of certain demonic holdings in our lives are a result of unforgiveness. I can recall the experience of a young lady we prayed for who was sexually abused by her father. Her condition became worse after every prayer session until the Holy Spirit revealed this to one of the brethren. She was confronted with the issue and, though it was difficult to do, her deliverance and healing began when she forgave herself first and then forgave her father. The choice is always ours to make. Many of us have been hurt in one way or another and have hurt others in the process. The pain of unforgiveness is always borne more by the one who is keeping the events and the sequence than the one who hurt us and has probably moved on. The golden rule, as Christ taught us, is still seventy times seven a day:

"Then came Peter to him, and said, Lord, how oft shall my brother sin against me, and I forgive him? 'Til seven times? Jesus saith unto

him, I say not unto thee, until seven times: but, until seventy times seven." (Matthew 18:21-22)

This is difficult to practice in a day, but yes that is what Christ taught us. If we learn to be Christ-like and allow Him to live through us, then we can say as He said: *"Father forgive them, for they don't know what they are doing."* This is what Stephen did in Acts Chapter 9. Not only will we create a godly room for ourselves to attract God's blessings but will also release those we forgive into their effective ministries like Paul the apostle. For many of us we have lost great moments and opportunities because of an unforgiving spirit and its seeds in us. ***Learn to let go and give to God. We are tried always, but we will overcome, Christ being our helper.***

I was confronted, on January 29 2006, by God in this manner. I can recall some prayers I wanted to pray and God asked me, "Who will answer you?" My answer was certainly, "You, Lord," but He said, "Forgive yourself and others and look ahead to what I want you to know." During these periods, I never shared my pain with anybody until God asked me to share with others. You may be the reason I have to write this history, as God wants you to move ahead. God has given me more incidences that prove this and I bless him for the opportunity to continue. Thank God for brothers and men like Mr Francis Yaw Poku, Reverend Ebenezer Nana Kwaku Anti, Dr Francis Agyeman-Yeboah (FAY), Ato Robertson and our sister Mrs Josephine Owusu-Agyemang, affectionately called Maame Joe. My prayer is that God will give you the heart and the grace to practise forgiveness.

I read the story of the great man John Osteen, the founder of Lakewood Church, Houston, Texas, in the book *Your Best life Ever* by his son Joel Osteen. I then realized that whatever happens is for a reason and a purpose and we must not lose sight of the vision but keep on with God's plan for our lives. Being unsuccessful in his first marriage, Osteen almost gave up and rescinded his faith. But, his decision to give up and settle for anything gave way to his response to God's calling and the great ministries and impact he has left is undoubtedly evidence of forgiving the past and moving on towards the vision. Today, the Osteen's ministries is one of God's local churches in America making waves and impact, because a man refused to allow his past experiences to deter him from moving on and trusting God to open doors. What would have happened if he had given up?

My greatest desire now is to do what God wants me to do. That is the only thing that will bring reward to us in this life and after. ***Don't ever consider failure as the end to your life, vision or dreams but rather a means to the end. As a man rightly put it, "it is just another way of learning to do it again."***

Don't give up till the race is won. The prize is yours when the victory is had. Jesus, our victor has already won and we must look up to Him to endure the cross – the wilderness – until we come out successfully. It doesn't matter how long it may take – be it days, months or years – there will be an end to it one day and God will bring you to the place of fulfillment.

Will God Answer You?

He answers us all the time. He directs us in His will. He shows us His ways but wants us to endure the cross. Did God forget Joseph when he was sold into slavery by his own brethren? What about when he was put into prison? I can recall the incident of King Saul trying to kill David after David had claimed victory for Israel. Daniel was led into the lion's den by his conviction to pray to God when it was outlawed. In all these stories, you can perceive God's silence in the situations, but my admonition to you is that He allows us to go through such times and training in order to fulfill His purpose in us. It is part of our wilderness training.

Never discount your experience, no matter how bitter it may be, for the Holy Spirit works it out for your good and it is necessary for our purpose on Earth. It may directly or indirectly relate to our training for an assignment on Earth.

Lessons from my Wilderness

Learning Not to Trust in Man

Sometimes we are confident and certain of promises, believing that they will materialize. We don't only trust the words, but also the people who spoke them, depending on their background and our relationship to them. We are trapped into believing them, even though we know of God's word that we should not trust in man. Some of their words may make it seem as if they will not fail. Man may fail but God cannot lie. How many times have we been disappointed by someone we were confident of? From this experience, I have learned to believe God through others and I am convinced that, until God touches the heart of a person, he cannot do anything for me. Therefore, trust no man.

Success in God

God does not see success by our kind of measurement. To Him, much is given, much is required. God has given to each one of us the ability to perform according to our capability. That is why it would be infantile to measure ourselves against one another because we are different. Ministries and personal goal setting should conform to our God-given potential and not our expectations. In the scripture, Josiah fulfilled his ministry because he did what was pleasing to God. It would be wrong to measure our success against one another without referring to ourselves. The best person to compare yourself to is you and what God has committed to your hands. Sometimes like King Saul, we think that we have achieved a lot by the success around us, forgetting that we have a specific assignment. (1 Samuel 15:18)

Paul rightly puts it in 2 Corinthians 10:12:

"For we dare not make ourselves of the number, or compare ourselves with some that commend themselves: but they measuring themselves

by themselves, and comparing themselves among themselves, are not wise."

It is just immature to do that. The parable of the talents shows how each receives talents according to their ability. **You will give an account of what you were given and not of what others received.**

In all that I have gone through, I acquired many useful lessons. A good student is the one who takes his lessons well and uses them to solve questions as they come to him. I always pray that I will note and never repeat the mistakes of the past. Sometimes, we may not have the opportunity to make amends and so we need to learn from others to avoid avoidable mistakes and learn to serve God in His way. Asking God for a fresh leaf will erase the past for you to move ahead. Again, don't allow anybody to blacklist you with the past.

"Therefore, if any man be in Christ, he is a new creation, the old is past, behold everything becomes new." (2 Corinthians 5:17) Satan will always use your past to intimidate you but we must consider it only as a lesson for us and the generations to come.

CHAPTER NINE

The Thirty and Forty Change

. . . .

In Life, the only thing that remains constant
is change. Either you embrace or it takes you
along if you refuse to acknowledge it.

. . . .

"And Joseph was thirty years old when he stood before Pharaoh King of Egypt. And Joseph went out from the presence of Pharaoh, and went throughout all the land of Egypt." (Genesis 41:46)

"And when he was full forty years old, it came into his heart to visit his brethren the children of Israel." (Acts 7:23)

"And when forty years were expired, there appeared to him in the wilderness of mount Sinai an angel of the Lord in a flame of fire in a bush." (Acts 7:30)

"Then God turned, and gave them up to worship the host of heaven; as it is written in the book of the prophets, 'O ye house of Israel, have ye offered to me slain beasts and sacrifices by the space of forty years in the wilderness?'" (Acts 7:42)

"David was thirty years old when he began to reign, and he reigned forty years." (2 Samuel 5:4)

"And Jesus himself began to be about thirty years of age, being (as was supposed) the son of Joseph, which was the son of Heli." (Luke 3:23)

"For the children of Israel walked forty years in the wilderness, til all the people that were men of war, which came out of Egypt, were consumed, because they obeyed not the voice of the Lord: unto whom the Lord sware that he would not shew them the land, which the Lord sware unto their fathers that he would give us, a land that floweth with milk and honey." (Joshua 5:6)

Numbers are of great significance. This is why dates are important. The essence of the day and night is not for nothing. God has a purpose for all that and we need to examine this against the background of our study. The number three stands for the Trinity. When the executive decision of the Trinity is reached, change is inevitable. Jesus died and rose up again on the third day. Thus, three thirty, 300 and the like have significance in the Bible and the history of life. The number four as in four, forty, 400, 4000 etc. represents a change in the Bible. Thus the examples of these men all had something to do with the changes associated with them and when they encountered these changes.

The number seven also stands for completeness. For example, God completed creation on the seventh day. Elisha asked Naaman to wash himself seven times and there are many other examples. The number eight is for a beginning. It starts after the cycle is complete, which is represented by seven.

One underlying truth of the men of the wilderness was the change that happened to them and its association with these figures. ***The change we so desire will certainly come at the right time.***

> *The change we so desire will certainly come at the right time.*

Job 14:14 says, *"If a man dies, can he live again, no all the days of my appointed time will I wait until my change comes."*

Change is inevitable. Everything in life is subject to change, except the word of God that is forever established. (Psalms 119:89) What you do with the change that comes to you will determine the level you go to. Your time of wilderness has an end. Most of us become desperate and worried as we ask ourselves when all this will come to pass. For the majority of us who also believe that we are equipped enough and want our coronation now, we forget that to every season there is a time and a purpose.

Joseph became a prime minister at the age of thirty. Likewise, David graduated from his wilderness training which took him to the bush and the palace, and he finally became the King of Israel at the age of thirty. Jesus started his Earthly ministry at the age of thirty and went through a forty-day journey of fasting, fulfilling and completing the processes of mankind. Moses had different encounters in fulfilling his calling at forty-year intervals. He fled Egypt at age forty, and had the wilderness experience and the bush encounter after another forty-year interval, that is, at the age of eighty. It took him another forty years with the Israelites in the wilderness. He died at the age of 120. The Israelites were delivered from Egypt after 430 years in slavery. It took them another forty years to get to the Promised Land. A look at Daniel's life and the prayer for the deliverance of the people was a completion of 400 years in captivity. Call all these coincidences and I will tell you of God's ultimate plan for mankind.

When the end of the thirties, the forties come to us, and then we will understand how a slave boy could become the Prince of Egypt and a prime minister. Pharaoh's daughter's son, the adopted son and a fugitive in Egypt became a deliverer, the shepherd boy who lived in the bush became the King of Israel, the captive in exile became a prince not only in one kingdom but all the reign of the kings of his time, and the carpenter's son became the King of kings and the Lord of lords.

The Transitional Period and What to Do

There is what we call the period of transition. This is your period of wilderness. If the timing has not come to pass, don't give up and lose hope. Child of God, you have got to rise up and raise your spirit, because a miracle is about to happen. Archbishop Duncan Williams of Action Chapel International, Accra Ghana, once said, **"The level of your expectation is the breeding ground for your unprecedented miracle."** What is important are the lessons you have acquired in the period of your wilderness experience and whether these lessons are worth showing to the world. As some disappointed God after their forty years of wilderness experience, the people of Israel failed to reach the Promised Land. Be this far from you. **Our dispensation does not have enough time to go through all the mistakes of the past, but God has used the examples of these ones to make us do better and perform more effectively."**

After Jesus had gone through thirty years of quiet ministry and forty days of wilderness testing, he fulfilled the principle of change in his life. Luke 4:21 confirms that now is the hour. After he returned from the wilderness, Jesus spoke this word:

"And he began to say unto them, 'This day is this scripture fulfilled in your ears.'"

Joseph experienced a change at the age of thirty. David finally became King of Israel at the age of thirty. Jesus started his ministry at the age of thirty. On the other hand, Moses intermittently encountered God at the age of forty, and forty years later was sent to deliver the people. The wilderness journey of the people he brought from Egypt took forty years. Daniel perceived that the 400 years of slavery was overdue and that it was time for the people to come out of slavery. He prayed to God to remember His promise because the change was due. Despite the significance of numbers, one thing is quite clear, that every wilderness training has an end. It shall surely come to pass someday. Therefore, don't lose hope but learn well your lessons.

The time for your change will come. The day for your lifting will come. The hour for your glorification will come. The period for the fulfilling of your scripture will come. Don't give up, because change for better is about to take place. No situation is permanent. Everything is subject to change and your change will come. Many of us will experience angelic visitations and in our period of change we will wonder and marvel about what and where God is taking us.

The Missing Gap

There is a period in walking with God called the "missing gap." This is a period when it seems that knowing all that God has in store for you with prophecies, convictions and the word of knowledge changes nothing. All these men went through such a time. Joseph, for instance, was pretty much aware of what was in store for him. The time lapse between the vision and the actualization of the dreams is the missing gap. You may actually experience other favors, but may not necessarily see what God is doing. You question when all this will come to pass. But the manifestation of the vision is near to you and is about to break forth as was told, rather than you may have imagined. Do not give up in between these periods. Hold on to the vision and persist till your thirty or forty comes. Draw inspiration from the men and women who have walked this way before. Ask anyone who has walked with God and has trusted God to bring to pass what He is doing and he will not hesitate to tell you of these periods. Sometimes your prayer may not seem enough and you may think God is a distance away. No, He is about to graduate you.

In school I was given a plaque with an inscription of a footprint that tells of our journey with God. This was an experience of a man that says, "One day he had a dream and was walking with God. When he started the journey, the footprints were two, that of him and God. As they journeyed far, he realized that the footprint had become one and he could not see the other. He was looking for the other one but could not understand what had happened. He asked God later where He went since he was not seeing Him in the journey. Then the Lord said He was carrying him on His shoulders and so the footprints he saw were for God and not the man."

Yes, at certain times, we come to a place where we feel that God has ignored us. We seem not to hear and experience the things that characterized our early walk with him. Think of Joseph in prison and compare it to how you sometimes feel alone. It appears that you are the only one making the journey. Prayers may not be enough for you, but understand that He has not forsaken you. I have been to that stage several times in my social life, marital life and whatever area you can think of. What we forget is that the mercies and the grace of God keep us each day of the journey until we come to a place of fruitfulness and satisfaction. With the Israelites, the pillar of fire and cloud was still keeping the distance between them and the Egyptians. ***Until such a time, keep on keeping on and don't give up.***

The wilderness is a place like that but the Promised land is just ahead of you after you have crossed your Jordan. You are close to the Promise Land and have the Host with you. The fact that you are not seeing Him does not mean He is not with you. Jesus himself came to a place in His life when He felt the Father had forsaken Him. In one breath, God had forsaken Him because of the sins of you and I, but the Father was also waiting to allow the son to endure the sufferings in order to glorify Him later. It's difficult to believe sometimes, but the truth is, He will never leave you nor forsake you. ***You cannot be glorified if you don't go through the sufferings of life with Him.*** Jesus said, if we want to reign with Him, then we must also suffer with Him. (2 Timothy 2:12)

Scripture Reference

Thy way is in the sea, and thy path in the great waters, and thy footsteps are not known. Thou leddest thy people like a flock by the hand of Moses and Aaron." (Psalm 77:19-20)

"So they did eat, and were well filled: for he gave them their own desire." (Psalm 78:29) God will give you your own manna in your period of wilderness and the good of the land when you get to the Promised Land.

"*Arise, walk through the land in the length of it and in the breadth of it; for I will give it unto thee. Then Abram removed his tent, and came and dwelt in the plain of Mamre, which is in Hebron, and built there an altar unto the Lord.*" (Gen 13:17-18) Whatever God has showed to you is evidence of what He is capable of giving to you.

"*For Judah prevailed above his brethren, and of him came the chief ruler; but the birthright was Joseph's.*" (1 Chronicles 5:2) Joseph's wilderness experience and endurance earned him the birthright of the sons of Jacob, though the least among them. What God will do with your life will not be determined by vote but by divine executive mandate.

"*Neither said they, 'Where is the Lord that brought us up out of the land of Egypt, that led us through the wilderness, through a land of deserts and of pits, through a land of drought, and of the shadow of death, through a land that no man passed through, and where no man dwelt?' And I brought you into a plentiful country, to eat the fruit thereof and the goodness thereof; but when ye entered, ye defiled my land, and made mine heritage an abomination.*" (Jeremiah 2:6-7). God is always faithful, what He has said, He will do it but we must not take Him for granted and sin against Him after He has made His ways known to us like He did for the Israelites.

CHAPTER TEN

The Trial of the 21st Century Generals

• •

The real knowledge of God is obtained
through an encounter with Him. A deeper
insight is revealed when we get closer.

• •

Our lives are under a microscope. We are tested on what we are hearing, reading, studying and teaching. We are going to be judged by them and will have little or no excuse should we fail to reach the high calling of the mark set for us. Our generation has a high standard set for it to achieve. We are in a better position than that of Moses, David, Daniel and the others because of the availability of their enormous experience. We have no excuse not to perform better.

"*Verily I say unto you, Among them that are born of women there hath not risen a greater than John the Baptist: notwithstanding he that is least in the kingdom of heaven is greater than he.*" (Matthew 11:11)

Great are the expectations both of the world and of God on us as His people. Remember we are all going to stand in judgment, but some may plead that they did not have enough information at their disposal, hence the mistakes they made. Even though that may not be an excuse, how can we in the 21st century and subsequent generations plead our case before God? It is about time we ready ourselves for God's use and serve our generation with a godly character. As it is written, David finished serving his generation. Jesus said, *"It will be more tolerable for Sodom and Gomorrah than for this generation."* (Luke 10:13-14)

Can you judge yourself with the statement from Apostle Paul that says, "I have fought the good fight of faith and finished the race?" Can you in confidence tell your end from your beginning and serve right and live faithfully to the end? Are you going to be one of the failures of the wilderness? Are you sure you can complete the race set for you?

You Are God's First Choice

As I went through the daily battles trying to understand why there were certain delays in my life and why I had gone through what I had, I almost came to the point of giving up. For many years, I lived my life for others and could not point to something specific of my own. Sometimes you don't get help from people into whose lives you have deposited so much time. As I walked and questioned myself about life in May 2005, the word of the Lord came explicitly to me: "Son, listen, you are a possibility and not a probability. You are not just like any ordinary person, despite how you may see yourself. Things don't just happen to you by chance, but rather according to my timetable. You may think that happenings around you make you but things don't make you." This changed my perspective as say it to myself every day.

Canaan is the place where God's promises are fulfilled in our lives – the place where God maximizes the potential of His people both individually and collectively. In the Old Testament, Canaan land was where God wanted the Israelites to live after He delivered them from their bondage in Egypt. They were to live there in faith and God would fulfill His promises to them.

Possessing your Canaan may not mean that when you travel from one place to the other, the Lord has prospered in you. Instead, it is when He accomplishes in you His desire and purposes, bringing you to a place of His sufficiency and satisfaction; abundance and peace, riches both spiritual and material, and making you a possessor and not a beggar. It is a place of complete obedience and submission to His will in which you can go where He sends you and fulfill His desire without a struggle.

A challenge is the purifier that refines and brings out the best in you. God has designed life such to makes all things work together for the good of us all. *Like gold in its unrefined state, so God picks us and refines us through the fire of life – the wilderness – to purge us of the impurities of Egypt until we become precious, shining and as desirable an ornament as gold in its final state.*

Lessons from the Past

Not all these men's deeds and actions are worthy of emulation. God makes us appreciate their strengths and weaknesses in order to draw good lessons. For instance, David had a good wilderness experience but failed to please God in all his ways. He made problems for himself and his household because he chose to live a self-centered life. He had more than one wife, hence the troubles in his own house. Failing to deal with his lustful desires brought unto him the punishment he suffered for killing Uriah.

Think about Moses and you will understand that, though he had promised to reach the land God had ask him to take the people to, he failed to reach the land. A simple act of disobedience that would have meant nothing to you mattered in the case of Moses and God. He knew so much of God in terms of his ways and should not have made that mistake. The majority of Christians displease God as in the case of Samson. When we all appear before God, it is possible to hear, "Sorry I don't know you." What a waste of time this would be to me! In fact, God is not surprised by the miracles we experience but rather interested in what He asks us to do. Some of the men's lessons, such as defying their challenges to hold on to the dreams received from God, are worth emulating whilst others are to be read about so that we will fall victim to the same things they committed. Some of the actions made them incur the displeasure of God.

Fasting and prayer was a sign of dependency and seeking direction before ministry.

"If thou be the son of God, command this stone to be turned into bread" was a test of Jesus's power and He did not need to show off. His personality and attitude was tested. Twenty-first Century Generals must learn to deal with the image of themselves and project God rather than their gifts and potential. In fact, we are not the originators of the power but only instruments for God's use.

The need to learn and depend on the Holy Spirit for direction is another important factor. It is also a period of appropriating the anointing and the potential in us.

Go Ahead and Don't Give Up

"Testing produces testimonies."

Tell me about your **mess** and I will tell you that you have a **message**. Tell me your **test** and **trials** and I will tell you, you have a **testimony**. Say to me that I have **failed**, and I will tell you that you are about to **fulfill** your task. In your **disappointment**, God has an **appointment** for you. In your **discouragement**, be **encouraged** to move ahead. The **bitter** situation is becoming **better** now. Our **brokenness** leads to God's **boldness** in us. **Fear** will give way to **faith** and much more.

There is more room for God in you after your wilderness experience. God intends for you the Promised Land, filled with honey, milk and much more. Literally speaking, it is the blessings of the Lord that makes a difference. The Hittites, Jebusites, and Girgashites lived on the land without realizing this blessing. (Deuteronomy 7:1) Apart from the physical evidence of fruitfulness on the land, they were only living as tenants until the real occupants came. Do not fret over God's promises and prophecies to you. Learn to live right, hear right, walk right and believe God will fulfill His promises. Remember the Earth is the Lord and the fullness thereof. He has prepared a place for you in the land of the living – ministry, marriage, education, career, and no one can deny you. As He has said, so will He do it also.

As 21st Century Generals, we must pass this test in the wilderness. We need to be encouraged by the experience of the fathers and *go ahead*. Face the situation, understand God's timing, wait for your turn, and never fret about the success of others. Remember, God's success is different from man's. Fulfill your dream, become a possessor and let the name of God be glorified.

I will meet you again as we examine God's prophetic word and how to make it work for you. See you on the other side.

I DID IT BY
PRAYER

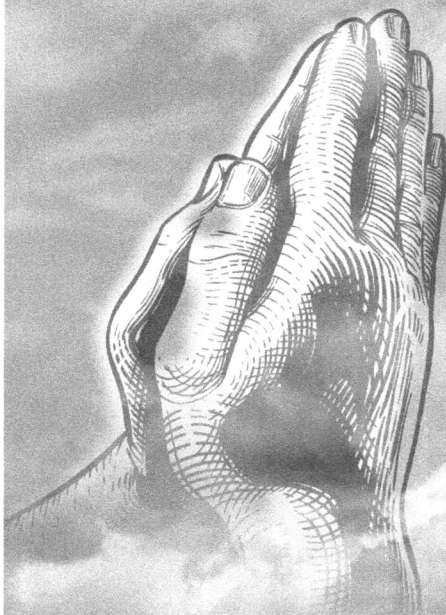

Gabriel Donkor

www.ingramcontent.com/pod-product-compliance
Lightning Source LLC
Chambersburg PA
CBHW072027040426
42447CB00009B/1767